Hans-Jürgen Warnecke

The Fractal Company

A Revolution in Corporate Culture

In Collaboration with Manfred Hüser

Translated by Maurice Claypole

With 85 Figures

Springer-Verlag
Berlin Heidelberg New York
London Paris Tokyo
HongKong Barcelona Budapest

Dr. h.c. mult. Dr.-Ing. Hans-Jürgen Warnecke

Professor of Industrial Manufacturing and Management
University of Stuttgart and Head of the Fraunhofer Institute
for Manufacturing Engineering and Automation (IPA)

ISBN 3-540-56537-X Springer-Verlag Berlin Heidelberg New York
ISBN 0-387-56537-X Springer-Verlag New York Berlin Heidelberg

© Springer-Verlag 1993
Printed in Germany

Cover design: Struve & Partner, Heidelberg and Otto Gann, Grafenau
Typesetting: Camera-ready by author;
Printing: Color-Druck Dorfi GmbH, Berlin; Binding: Lüderitz & Bauer, Berlin
60/3020   5 4 3 2 1 0   Printed on acid-free paper

Foreword to the English Edition

This book first appeared in German in 1992 under the title, *"Die Fraktale Fabrik"*. The considerable interest which it has aroused, in particular in business and scientific circles, has encouraged me to make the discourse and ideas it contains available to a readership beyond the confines of Germany.

For this edition the title, *"The Fractal Company"* has been specifically chosen to reflect the fact that the deliberations which are limited here to aspects of manufacturing are equally valid for the company as a whole. This is also intended as a contribution to the interdisciplinary exchange of ideas for which there is currently an unprecedented need. However, since it is primarily those in positions of responsibility in the manufacturing industry whose work will be most likely to benefit from it, the following text makes reference to the *"Fractal Factory"*, which is a direct translation of the German title.

At the same time the need arises to develop the concept further in areas which could only be touched on within the scope of this book. I would therefore greatly welcome an exchange of views with interested parties in science and industry.

I should like to take this opportunity to mention Maurice Claypole, to whom I owe my gratitude for the speed and care with which he undertook the translation of the German text into English.

Hans-Jürgen Warnecke   Stuttgart, February 1993

Foreword to the German Edition

The tremendous economic development which has been taking place in particular in the USA, Europe and Japan over the last 100 years has made a high standard of living possible for a great many people. The instigator and agent of this development, namely the manufacturing industry, has been producing material goods at ever more cost-effective prices. The key to this success was the introduction of mass production with mechanized manufacturing facilities using conveyor belts together with a greater division and simplification of labor, so that falling production costs and prices went hand in hand with an increase in purchasing power. Capital investment in production machines with an increasingly higher degree of automation was rewarded by an increase in productivity. The methods used to organize a factory and manage its employees have constantly been refined, whereby business and science have mutually profited from each other. Guidelines or paradigms remained constant and the assumption for the future was that more powerful information technology would transform data processing into information processing and finally into knowledge engineering. This would lead to improved scheduling and greater control over manufacturing processes and even the complex system of the factory would sooner or later become largely automated. This gave rise to the image of the factory of the future.

But it is precisely the intense study of this approach, encapsulated in the term CIM, the integration by computer of all the processes within a factory, which has led to doubts, perhaps less with regard to the feasibility of continued technical advances as to their expediency. The deterministic view of the world on which this is based, dealing with the familiar relationships between cause and effect or with those relationships accessible after the appropriate research work has been done, is not adequate, since it is only valid for certain limited aspects of reality. In modern science, particularly in physics, this insight has now received general acceptance; the mathematician knows the difficulty verging on impossibility of quantifying and calculating a system with numerous elements bearing multiple, often non-linear relationships to one another. It is only possible to try to create order from chaos by working with probabilities, approximations and fuzzy concepts. In practice, this means that only the most pressing problem can be dealt with in each instance, although quite a different one may be appropriate tomorrow and although views as to the priorities to be set can also differ considerably.

However, if we accept this as a reality which can not be quantified and modelled any more effectively in the foreseeable future and possibly never will be, then we must amend our approaches and act accordingly. The fast global information and communications systems that we now have give us an insight into a turbulent and complex world the dynamic nature of which calls into question every position so far adopted. This means that we must also rethink our previous guidelines with regard to company organization, staff management and manufacturing structures. We find ourselves in the midst of a revolution. Existing forms of performance optimization have attained a high degree of sophistication; they have therefore reached a state in which an increase in effort, however great, offers only diminishing marginal utility. New attempts are expressed in key words and methods such as strategic alliances, complexity reduction, concentration of core areas, reduction in the vertical range of manufacture, overhead value analysis, segmentation, creation of production cells, group technology or lean management. The question is whether the variety of solutions on offer have any factors in common which can be integrated into a holistic approach.

The term "Fractal Factory" represents an attempt to reduce the considerations and phenomena in science and industry to a common denominator. Above all, it is a question of stimulating awareness, which is a precondition for bringing about a change of thinking. I am aware that the term "fractal" is not immediately accessible, since it is still a relatively new term in science. It was coined to describe organisms and structures in nature, which arrives at multiple and complex solutions, albeit task-specific ones, by using a small number of self-imitating elements. The essential characteristics of fractals are self-organization, self-optimization and dynamics. So, too, must a factory be seen as a living organism. In a market economy whose goal is the satisfaction of needs, which is itself a very human-oriented aspect, manufacturing companies are particularly subject to a very hard process of selection comparable to that found in nature. This must and will remain so if the market economy is to continue to achieve its original goals and is not to be distorted by other, overambitious objectives, which could result, for example, in a stifling of the necessary structural modifications. A market economy works according to the same principles as fractals: self-organization and self-optimization in small, rapidly changing areas of regulation. Each is useful to the others and also benefits from them.

Manufacturing must be regarded as a service. A manufacturing company must be structured internally and externally according to this principle. The division of labor and a strictly operational approach within a company have caused the notion of service and direct communication with the consumer, whether it is a colleague within the organization or an external customer, to be lost sight of. For too many employees the relationship between the company and the outside world is not relevant. We are in urgent need of direct communication on the horizontal level of performance instead of instructions and information being transmitted through vertical levels of hierarchy. Fractals communicate directly with their counterpart fractals amongst sub-contractors or customers. Fractals can be distributed throughout the whole world. They select the relevant methods, for example for scheduling and process control, through self-organization and employ the machines and computers appropriate to the completion of their task. This continues to provide us with a wide variety of solutions. This does not make it any easier to manage and to structure an enterprise; it makes it more difficult. Increased demands are placed on individual employees or groups of employees. Objectives are set, coordination is obtained and adjustments are made via networks. Establishing and managing such networks is the managerial, organizational and technical challenge of the future.

The author does not claim to be saying anything radically new in this book; rather it is an attempt to place tendencies that have been identified and case examples from practice within the framework of an overall context and to derive from them a holistic approach. In this, it is his aim to contribute to the awareness and sense of direction in the current third industrial revolution.

A large part of this book was written with the assistance of Manfred Hüser. This applies both to the contents and to the layout of the text and the illustrations. I owe my gratitude to him for his exceptional contribution and commitment.

A number of other members of the Fraunhofer Institute for Manufacturing Engineering and Automation (IPA) formed themselves into a working party which received ideas with great enthusiasm and contributed to their development. My thanks also go to them and I would like to single out for mention by name Hermann Kühnle, who is in charge of the Institute's main department, Corporate Planning and Control, and also Gerhard Spengler, who undertook editorial tasks in a free-lance capacity.

I extend my thanks to the publishers, Springer Verlag, for receiving the manuscript and publishing the work in such a short time. I hope that the response from the readers, whether they feel themselves addressed directly by this book as members of science and industry or whether they peruse it as interested observers, is a positive one.

Hans-Jürgen Warnecke   Stuttgart, May 1992

Preface

Whenever we think of industry, we think of its products. They reflect our wishes and fears, judgements and prejudices. The widely held view that industrial products such as automobiles, airplanes, computers and television sets, ball pens and photocopiers have dramatically changed our world is quite correct. However, this idea contains at best only half of the truth. From a historical point of view it is not the products but rather the methods of their production that have shaped the history of our culture and not only this. Woven garments were worn in antiquity, but it was the mechanical loom that first made textiles into a consumer product. The methods of producing iron and steel, which were developed in pre-Christian days in the Near East, have probably influenced the course of history more than we would assume from the emphasis placed by historians on battles and rulers. It is therefore appropriate to the way we see ourselves today that one of the most important areas of engineering science investigates the evolution of production techniques (EPT). The present book arises from such research.

The process of industrialization which started in the previous century arose from the exploitation of the steam engine, as considerably improved by James Watt. In other words, it was the result of a change in production technology. Since the power used to drive the machinery could at first be transmitted only by mechanical means, all production machines driven by a single steam engine had to be concentrated in one place. This led to the development of the factory. To this day, its trademark remains the smoke stack associated with the boiler. Industrialization was the result of a change in the significance of energy as a production factor. Energy had always been a part of every manufacturing process but it could now be made available in greater quantities and at almost any location.

In the second industrial revolution another production factor acquired dominance: labor. This was mainly because of the increasing demands for qualifications placed on, and largely met by, the working population. This established the basis for a hitherto unknown increase in net output per man-hour but also laid the foundations for the method of acquiring a share in the resultant profits, namely the power of strike. From 1950 to 1975 the per capita income in real terms in the

Federal Republic of Germany rose by 300 per cent, that is, by more than ten times the amount of growth in comparable earlier periods. We were and are living in an age of rationalization during which production techniques in most branches of industry have undergone radical change. It is time to realize that the successes of the first industrial revolution, that is of industrialization itself, is approaching saturation point.

So far, this has barely been evident because in the period since the seventies we have been experiencing a third era of change in manufacturing processes, the age of automation. The impetus for this came from the fact that electronic data processing is constantly becoming more economical. This accorded a new and far-reaching significance to a production factor, which like energy or labor had always been present: information, or rather the transformation of information within the manufacturing process. When we occupy ourselves with this phenomenon, an abstract image results:

According to this view a factory is a system in which a ramified energy stream controlled by information acts upon a material stream, also controlled by information, in such a way that raw materials are converted into the final product.

This image tells us nothing about the nature of information transformation and for this reason not every type of automation necessitates the application of electronic data processing.

This is the scenario in which the "Fractal Factory" should be seen. It presupposes that the process of industrialization, i.e. the economically and ecologically optimized use of energy, has been fully completed. It completes the second industrial revolution and accords to the factor of labor, in addition to an increased technical competence, a share of the responsibility in the factory's activities in an expanded area of organization. Furthermore, it creates a new quality of qualifications for human beings working in a factory.

The means suggested for achieving the "Fractal Factory" arise from the school of thought of the third industrial revolution. Automation can involve making a process run without the (usually regulating) intervention of humans. Automation in the wider sense, however, also means the establishment of systems which are self-regulating. The basic idea of the fractal is the creation of self-regulating organizational working groups, each within its own area of competence. The coordination of the input and output values of the fractal is achieved by means of the superimposition of a computer assisted information and communication system.

However well the idea of the "Fractal Factory" fits into the contemporary EPT scenario, its greater significance lies in the new dimension it lends to our view of ourselves, and to the sense of achievement and self-fulfilment experienced by the individuals concerned.

The "Fractal Factory" not only creates factories within the factory, but entrepreneurs within the enterprise. It is appropriate to the self-image of the Westerner. It can transform his very individuality into the success factor of our working environment.

Otto H. Schiele   Cologne, April 1992

Professor Schiele is President of the German Federation of Industrial Co-operative Research Associations "Otto von Guericke" (AiF). He was Director of KSB, Frankenthal, and from 1983 to 1987 President of the German Machinery and Plant Manufacturers Association (VDMA).

Contents

1. Survival in a Turbulent Environment

There is no denying that uncertainty is currently running high in the business community, whilst the economic situation is sending shivers of disquiet through the public at large.

Anyone who closely follows the debates in industrial management circles can see that there is a growing need for new direction. In particular, increasing attention is being paid to questions relating to the future of the international division of labor and the right factory location. In this respect, we find ourselves focussing more and more on the competitive strength of Japanese industry. The original cause of the general commotion was a now almost legendary publication by the Massachusetts Institute of Technology (MIT) on the future of the automobile industry. In this study, production methods were subjected to a worldwide comparison with results that were far from flattering for those who had originally invented the automobile or had contributed to its widespread distribution (fig. 1).

All over the world, industry is looking for new direction

MIT emphasizes Japan's lead in automobile manufacture

This lack of direction is also manifest in the fact that at the present time a large number of companies have put their proposed automation projects 'on the back burner'. 'Lean production' is now in vogue, often without a clear understanding of what this means or how it is to be achieved. However, one thing is certain: lean production is no substitute for automation. The fact that some of the Japanese companies included in the comparison are even less automated than their European competitors can not be taken as a guiding principle.

Lean production is neither a panacea nor an alternative to automation

The solution is not to be found by visiting Japan

Computer integration and automation alone are not enough: diminishing marginal utility

Admittedly, a comparison of significant ratios is indeed disturbing. But it is worth remembering that some years ago certain figures appearing in a number of studies resulted in an immediate flurry of activity. German businessmen and engineers took off in droves for the Far East and the USA in search of the secrets of success.

This burst of activity occurred during a period when discussion amongst production specialists was dominated by the subject of 'computer integration'. With the consequent introduction of electronic data processing and the automation of all areas of production and service, companies deemed themselves to be well equipped to face international competition. It seemed that locational disadvantages could once again be overcome. The tremendous effort, including the intellectual effort, involved in this wave of integration has hardly been assimilated, and already the next challenge is looming ahead.

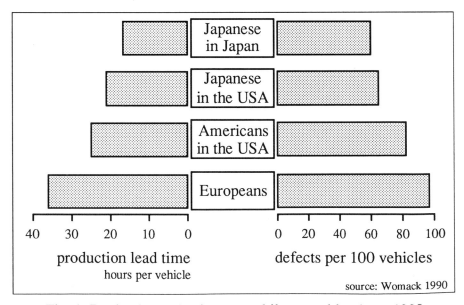

Fig. 1: Production ratios in automobile assembly plants 1989

However, before we succumb to panic we should try to ascertain what the basis of success, or rather of failure, actually is. Originally, a great deal of discussion centered on cost advantages, but these would not have any substantial effect unless low costs were accompanied by high quality. In time, innovations entered the field of view and with these, new discoveries were very quickly poured into new products and markets. Significant examples of this can be found in consumer electronics (video recorders and cameras) or communications devices (fax machines, mobile telephones). In any case, the popular explanatory approach pointing to labor costs and production times are only a very weak excuse for the differences in the competitive factors of cost, quality and speed (fig. 2).

In some branches of industry Japan has the edge in price, quality and speed

Production times and labor costs are not everything

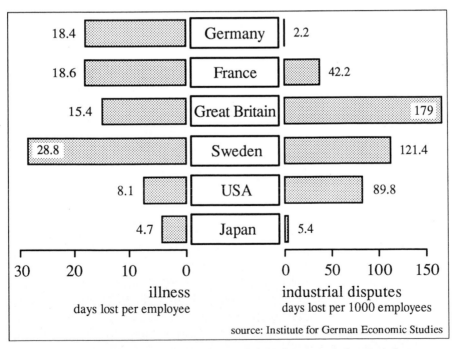

Fig. 2: Comparison of average national rates of absenteeism

Strategic thinking: market share first, profit margin second

Long-term strategic thinking and giving market shares priority over profit, which itself is generated automatically after a time, to say nothing of the commitment and intensity of work on the part of employees, are further elementary factors of success.

Planning has its limitations

The most striking feature of our economic system is its multiformity. Its superiority over all alternatives bearing a strong planning component has become evident in recent years and bears witness to the unpredictability inherent in the combination of all elements. This system behavior may be termed chaotic, the system environment turbulent. Even the most carefully constructed models which have been devised to describe the situation are basically inadequate. Consequently, the competitive strategies of firms operating in this environment assume very

There are many different strategies for success

different appearances. The range of possibilities between the most extreme positions is legion, the complexity of the model is exploding and a closed representation of all conceivable variations remains unattainable. The manufacturing strategy of a company can be seen in a similar light. Here too, extreme positions can be identified, but any number of individual strategies can be located in between. Survival entails finding one's way in this chaos and developing the correct strategy for one's own purposes.

Work ethic is part of success

As is so often the case, an in-depth study of one's supposed opponent ought to be of some help. And this opponent can easily be identified: Japan. Experts vie with each other with their intimate knowledge and analytical studies of Japan, although not all assertions serve to clarify the picture. Virtually all accounts place the work ethic of the Japanese firmly in the foreground. A further favorite explanation points to the activities of the Ministry of International Trade and Industry in Japan, MITI, which promotes cooperation between competing companies, scientists and research establishments as well as between politicians and banks in key technical and economic areas. The products are then manufactured and sold on the large, homogeneous domestic market under conditions of keen competition amongst Japanese companies. Subsequently, they are exported cut-price in order to open up the market, first to the USA and then to Europe.

Is MITI a model of industrial policy-making?

It is the behavior of the individual within the group or within the totality of business activity, the constant striving for improvement by employees, which is seen by many experts as a decisive indication of quality. We have already adopted the Japanese term 'KAIZEN' for this, without really knowing how this can be made into a natural component of company activity (fig. 3). In the literature and books on the subject there is either very little or nothing at all to be found under this heading.

KAIZEN, the constant improvement process, brings success

A German head of division in a Japanese-run company in Western Germany described this method to me as being extraordinarily effective.

KAIZEN: *constant and gradual improvements in all areas and on all levels.*

- doing little things better
- always being better tomorrow than today
- setting and maintaining constantly higher standards
- regarding everybody as a customer

Masaaki Imai

Fig. 3: KAIZEN - the continuous improvement process

*One way to
success:
implementing
improvement
suggestions
immediately*

Employees amongst themselves, but also staff across hierarchical boundaries, constantly monitor and check each other's efficiency. They exchange suggestions for improvement. And moreover, they put good ideas into practice instead of, as is often the case with us, regarding them as criticism and taking offence. In our companies such things are often not even mentioned, but are tolerated over long periods 'for the sake of peace and quiet'.

*The Japanese are
perfectionists*

In Japan, hierarchical structures are quite pronounced and are still closely related to the principle of seniority. If it really is true that the individual, even in a minor subordinate position, is already encouraged through tradition and education to play a constructive role in the community, then this will naturally have a major effect on the whole unit. But our distinct individuality prevents us from achieving these results so easily. The insider referred to above was fascinated, but also rather shocked, by his experiences in a Japanese company (fig. 4).

*Japanese firms
can both shock
and fascinate us*

*Speed brings
returns*

In recent years Japanese industry has been rapidly launching new models. In some cases changes to the models were merely cosmetic, but in many cases they were of a fundamental nature. By taking the lead in terms of timing and speed, the Japanese were able to consolidate their market position, which finally resulted in trade frictions. But it is becoming increasingly obvious that, quite apart from wasting important resources, this also led to a rapid fall in profits. Now MITI is issuing instructions to proceed more slowly. This will not, however, make companies lose their ability to innovate rapidly, but is more likely to result in more far-reaching innovations at longer

*No all-clear from
MITI*

intervals. So this development must not be interpreted as an all-clear.

Of course these brief observations do not pretend to be a complete summary of all of the complex events which have led to the current success of the Japanese in worldwide competition. But it is possible to draw one conclusion: *Now is the time to seize the initiative* further trips to Japan with the object of finding the recipe for success are no substitute for independent thoughts, decisions and actions. To protect our future, we must strive to develop forward-looking structures appropriate to our *We have lost the intellectual edge* own situation. Above all, there is one thing we must avoid in future: failing to put into practice our own knowledge and thoughts before they come back to us from elsewhere. Nor is it any

"In Japanese companies perverse economies prevail: a new pencil is only handed out on return of the stump of the old one."

"In management no compression of performance is striven for. There are no objections to a manager having a nap at his desk."

"Top management is integrated into the KAIZEN process."

"The standards used to assess employees are based on virtues such as
- cleanliness,
- tidiness,
- discipline,
- punctuality."

"No effort is too great when it is a matter of improving performance: desks are cheap junk, whereas office chairs are only of the very best."

"When there is a problem, the whole team gets together immediately and does not break up again until the problem is solved."

"The Japanese do not think in terms of performance, but of processes."

"There are no guilty parties."

"The highest guiding principle is the well-being of the company."

"A Japanese superior is never completely satisfied with the performance of his team."

"Criticisms are never aired directly, but expressed unequivocally in a roundabout way."

"Creativity derives from striving for quality. The Japanese are perfectionists."

Fig. 4: Observations made in a Japanese company in Germany

Today's extensive problems need holistic solutions

Even with lean production we are on the losing side because our competitors have achieved a high degree of sophistication with the method

It is futile to hope that the Far East will adopt Western values and structures

use counting and comparing the number of industrial robots or other automatic systems on each side or taking the degree of automation encountered in competing organizations as a yardstick. The time has come to realize that we are confronted by a technical, organizational and social challenge that can only be met by taking a holistic approach. Once we get caught in the vicious circle of looking to the competition to find the solution to our problems, instead of looking to ourselves, then we end up directing all our energies towards imitating existing solutions and will therefore continue to take second place.

Today, Western industrial nations find themselves in an extremely difficult position and this often gives rise to the image of a gloomy future, further nurtured by scenarios of the demise of whole branches of industry. We have already experienced such developments first hand, so this should make us act in a responsible way. Hoping that an increasing westernization of our Asian trading partners will bring their manufacturing conditions into line with ours gets us nowhere. On the contrary, it is a smoke screen used as an excuse for doing nothing.

However, in view of the turbulent changes in the environment, being apathetic and ignoring the problems are just as inappropriate as actionism or rapid imitation. The latter is currently taking on grotesque proportions. Only recently a plan has been established to build a 'Japanese factory' in Germany. Surely this can not be the right way; it is bound to end in technological imitation, which is obviously not a sensible strategy for Germany's export-oriented industry.

So what can be done? The first and most important step must be to regain the initiative. Only if we have the courage of our convictions and make an in-depth study of our own strengths and weaknesses will we be able to lead the field in the acquisition and application of knowledge.

We must seize back the initiative; the enemy that unites us is "out there"; it is not the colleague within

Pessimistic views of the future are often symptomatic of a fear of change. But we will be confronted with changes whatever happens and will be forced to discard familiar habits and practices. The history of industry is laden with examples of the coming and going of technologies, professional categories, organizations and business enterprises.

Fear and complacency must be overcome

The pace of innovation in organizational matters seems to be picking up lately. As is the case with new products, there is no longer time for a long and well-ordered life cycle. Manufacturing systems are becoming more and more dynamical and a factory can therefore not be allowed to "settle", but must be subjected to constant modification in the light of changing conditions. Persistent striving for improvement is probably the only kind of continuity a manufacturer needs. This is a possible clue to the lack of direction we observed at the outset; the speed of innovations and the proliferation of specialist areas involved are a major obstacle to the formulation of objectives. What we are experiencing are the multicausal effects of multivariable factors, a complexity of almost unmanageable proportions. We are in a race against time which also affects management and organizational design.

Dynamics in corporate development: organizations can not be static

Multicausal effects and multivariable factors = insuperable complexity

If there is a lesson to be learned from previous structural changes, it is that all attempts to resist the necessary modifications are doomed to

We must heed the warnings. Inaction can be fatal

failure. The Swiss and German watch and clock industries were once proud of their mechanical parts, the precision of which was unparalleled throughout the world. Their refusal or inability to appreciate and act upon developments affecting their own business led to the demise of the entire industry. This is all the more regrettable since the relevant know-how continues to be in demand, but no longer for watches and clocks.

Fear of change is nothing new

Of course, a discussion about the effects of technical developments is nothing new, as the following newspaper article from the year 1818 shows. At the time, the German states were feeling the brunt of the process of industrialization taking place in Britain:

A 19th century prophecy: industrialization will put millions on the streets

"A machine often makes the work of a thousand people unnecessary and puts the profits ... into the hands of a single person. With each new improvement made to a machine a family loses its breadwinner; each newly constructed steam engine multiplies the number of beggars and it is to be expected that soon all the wealth will be in the hands of a few thousand families, whereas the rest of the population will be reduced to the state of beggars in their servitude.

Is it not a cause for deep lament in each friend of man that it can, and probably must, come to this? We are of the opinion that the damage which our trade will suffer as a result of English mechanization, although it may hurt us, can be borne more easily than the pressure which would be caused by producing gauze in overmanned factories, which would fill Germany with three or four million beggars."   [Kölnische Zeitung 1818]

One may ask oneself why it is so difficult to adapt to changing circumstances and why this does not usually take place until it is too late. One explanation, in addition to the obvious human fear of change, is that design engineers are particularly prone to strive for perfection. They expect a good solution to be durable and believe that a great deal of effort must be spent on refining it, otherwise it will not last. Such a linear approach gives birth to a kind of determinism which is far removed from reality. But to survive we must embrace the whole of reality and act confidently, with clear objectives, and quickly.

Striving for perfection can lead to overcomplicated solutions

Linear, deterministic thinking is inadequate

2. Manufacturing - Yesterday, Today and Tomorrow

Changes through industrial revolutions

> "The mechanization which is on the march torments and disturbs me; it is rolling upon us like a storm, slowly, slowly; but it has assumed its course, it will come and strike."
>
> Goethe, Wilhelm Meister

'Technology' is over 200 years old

In 1790, Johann Beckmann, who taught economics in Göttingen, first used the term "technology" to denote a comprehensive description of the science of manufacturing processes in the various trades, the 'useful arts'. He laid down his thoughts in the work, 'Guideline to Technology or On the Science of Crafts, Factories and Manufactories, primarily those directly concerned with Agriculture, Policing and Cameral Science'.

Machines started a revolution

The years between 1750 and 1850 saw the advent of many technical innovations which brought about the transition from purely manual labor to mechanized manufacturing. The hallmark of this *First Industrial Revolution,* which started in England, was the increasing number of production machines of all kinds. The increased power requirement involved was met by the improved dual-chamber steam engine developed by James Watt around 1776.

The shortage of wood as a fuel and construction material led to the use of pit coal as a source of power and iron as a raw material. Iron also had better mechanical properties. The need therefore arose for processes, machines and tools which satisfied the demand for economical manufacturing and products made to the greatest possible precision. This period also saw the development of lathes and drills, mechanical planes and milling machines complete with mechanically operated tools. Forming techniques also benefited from the general upsurge. Mechanical forging hammers and rolling mills for the manufacture of metal sheets and profiles (e.g. railway tracks) entered the production arena. All such machines were driven by belts attached to a central power source, usually a steam engine.

Products, materials, tools, processes and machines interact to create progress

The steam engine increased productivity dramatically

For the transport of raw materials, semi-finished products and finished articles, transport systems had to be improved and highways extended, which had a lasting effect on civil engineering and urban development.

The breakthrough of mechanized technology came first in Great Britain in the then significant textile industry. Steady growth resulted in bottlenecks in the processing of raw materials which could not be overcome by existing technology and methods of production (needlework, homeworking). This provided the impetus for the development of spinning machines and mechanical looms.

The birth of mechanized production; the loom

The mass production of textiles brought about further changes and a persistent upsurge in many areas of commerce and technology. Radical changes followed at an explosive pace compared to the previous rate of technical change. The origins of the large-scale chemical industry can likewise be traced back to the mass production of textiles. Suitable agents for cleansing fibres, bleaching wool and dying cloths had to be made available in large

The mass production of textiles was the impetus for numerous technical innovations

*Science was
always one step
behind techno-
logical develop-
ments*

quantities. And the same period saw the introduction of town gas made from pit coal.

Most inventions of this period were made without the direct intervention of science. They were the fruits of the labors of inventors and engineers who had usually acquired the necessary theoretical knowledge autodidactically. Only hesitantly did academic science turn its hand to technical development work, and the engineering sciences which grew out of this did not receive recognition as such until the beginning of the 20th century.

*Management
science and socio-
logy were the
repair shop of the
working world*

At the time no-one was concerned about the effects of new technology on man and his environment. Child labor was the rule; overlong working days and a heavy work load coupled with squalid living conditions in industrial towns resulted in an above-average mortality rate amongst factory workers, as is revealed by a census taken in the year 1831. These conditions led to conflict and ended in hard-fought industrial disputes. The workers, citizens with no rights at the outset, acted for the first time as a coherent group. From these beginnings labor unions and social legislation sprang.

*Pauperization
theories were the
response to intol-
erable conditions*

"As a result of all this working men grow old before their time. Most of them are no longer fit for work at 40. A few manage to work to the age of 50. This is due not only to general physical debility but also to the failing eyesight which affects mule spinners. They have to watch closely a bank of fine parallel moving threads, and this must place a great strain on the eyes. Of 1,600 workers employed in several factories in Harpur and Larnak, only ten were over the age of 45."

[Friedrich Engels 1845]

One of the most crucial developments in manufacturing technology to date has been the
decentralization of the power source made
possible by the internal combustion engine
(patent application by Rudolf Diesel on
February 27, 1892), as well as by the dynamo
and the electric motor. These inventions
provided the means to multiply the productivity
of the workforce by installing power sources at
each workplace. We refer to this explosion of
mechanization as the *Second Industrial Revolution*. For practical purposes, it started in the
United States, increasing incomes throughout
the population whilst at the same time reducing
costs and prices.

*Technological
innovation always
proceeds from a
central solution to
decentralized
general
availability*

The Second Industrial Revolution was dominated by a megatrend: automation, which
initially entailed combining the individual
manufacturing processes into a comprehensive
chain of production stages. In this respect the
production lines of Henry Ford (1863-1947) in
Detroit were epochal. He installed a production
line for automobiles even before the First World
War. On these lines the workpiece was transported through a continuous-flow system to
each production stage at a rhythm calculated to
achieve the greatest possible economies in such
a way that work at them could take place simultaneously. At the end of the production line the
end-product emerged: the "Tin Lizzy", a car
which even the assembly line worker himself
could afford - an unheard-of luxury at the time.
During the period of the Second Industrial
Revolution the quantity of products manufactured was one of the most important parameters; mass-production was in its heyday.

*Mass production
led to automation
and the formation
of process chains*

*A pilot factory: the
Ford plant in
Detroit*

Parallel to automation on the material side,
information processing tools were developed to

Mass production permits the automated flow of material and information

control manufacturing processes, at first on the basis of human intervention and then later partly removed from the immediate control of the operator. Such largely automated systems were developed especially quickly in the chemical industry. In time, however, no industry remained untouched by the long arm of automation.

Even mass production did not make machines all-powerful

Automated mass production also made new demands on people. Today we know that the fears of the prophets of doom, who saw man as becoming merely an appendage of the all-powerful machine, have not been substantiated. In spite of all backlashes and crises, economic performance has continued to improve throughout the course of the past decades, and with it the standard of living of the individual.

Mass production created wealth and prosperity but also tension and ecological problems

However, this development has also had its darker side, from the problem of the global prosperity gap and the threat to the eco-system to the merciless exploitation of valuable natural resources.

With the development of the microprocessor we finally see a decentralization of 'intelligence', which enables manufacturing processes to be automated still further. Its main characteristic lies in the delegation of decisions to programmable machines. This type of automation is still in its infancy and we therefore find ourselves in the midst of the *Third Industrial Revolution*, which, like the second, is based on German inventions but is being promoted mainly by the USA and Japan.

The hallmark of the First Industrial Revolution was the transformation of the trades and agriculture into industrial work. The workers released by the tremendous increase in agricultural production (today they only amount to about three percent of the working population) were largely assimilated by the Second Industrial Revolution through the creation of menial jobs for semi-skilled workers. Increased productivity in all areas of manufacturing - less so in offices and administration - was due mainly to mechanization, which multiplied and cheapened the long-term physical efficiency of a human being of about only 80 watts.

Today we see decisions being delegated to machines

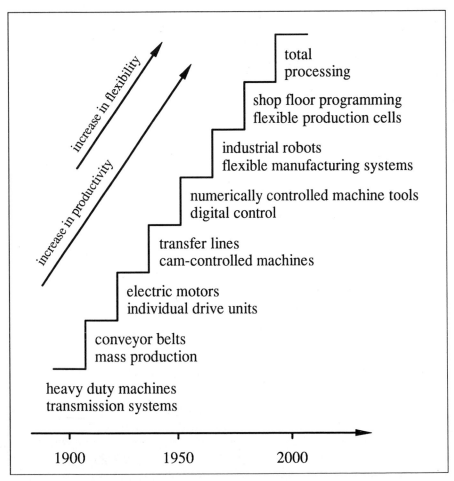

Fig. 5: Development stages in manufacturing technology

Machines are faster and more accurate; man is slower and less accurate, but more creative

The hallmark of the Third Industrial Revolution is an increase in productivity through multiplication and acceleration of human mental capacity with the aid of electronic computing and storage systems. It is typical of these 'machines' that they are capable of extremely accurate and very rapid computation and decision processes. The human brain is many times slower in comparison, but on the other hand, each switch and storage cell is networked with many times more inputs and outputs, enabling parallel operation and association, in other words creativity: a decisive and probably permanent distinction between humans on the one hand and machines and robots on the other.

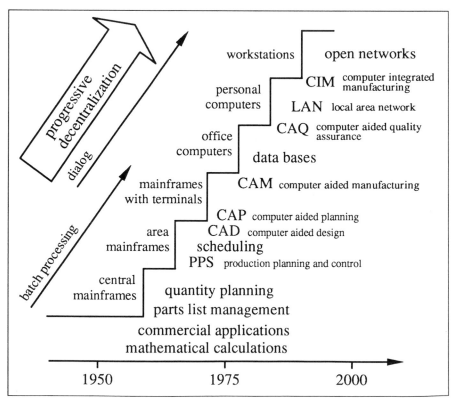

Fig. 6: Information processing in manufacturing

Finally, industry is heading unmistakably down the same road as agriculture. The number of employees required to ensure the supply of material goods is constantly falling. Structured unemployment and the transformation and disappearance of whole groups of professions are once again noticeable as side effects.

Fewer and fewer workers are needed to ensure the supply of material goods

One feature which all industrial revolutions have in common is a tendency away from centralization (steam engine, data processing center) to decentralization (electric motor, stand-alone computer, workstation). Furthermore they all tend to spread throughout the world in an irresistible wave of progress.

Innovations eventually become available throughout the world

Technical and scientific progress moves in two directions: on the one hand new scientific knowledge creates new products and processes whilst on the other hand new demands generate new discoveries (fig. 7). At the present time demand is being stimulated more and more through social developments and legislation, as for example in the case of renewable energy resources or environmental technology and waste disposal. So we have reason to hope that instead of being an added burden to the economy, new products, market opportunities and jobs will result.

The interplay between needs and knowledge

Energy consumption per capita of population and consumption of raw materials, and indirectly this applies to waste too, have long been the yardstick by which the affluence of a nation and the strength of its economy have been measured. We have now quite rightly learned not to regard this ratio as a significant indicator. The specific consumption of materials and energy must and will fall with increased 'intelligence' in products and manufacturing.

The specific consumption of raw materials will fall

Characteristic ratios are losing their importance

As obvious as this verdict may seem today, 25 years ago a highly-regarded publication derived its performance data and future expectations for an industrial nation from the factors, head of population, energy consumption and steel production [Seitz 1991]. Perhaps it is one of the ironies of world history that, measured by the yardsticks of the fifties (heavy industry), the

---

"Not only do new products and processes arise as a result of new scientific discoveries, but also new scientific discoveries result from new demands."

technical and scientific knowledge about methods and solutions \ market knowledge about goals and demands seen as tasks	still undiscovered market demand	latest (possibly newly created) market demand	known market demand
knowledge not yet acquired about technical and scientific methods and solutions	basic research	market research "demand pull"	traditional solutions
latest knowledge about technical and scientific methods and solutions (e.g. hydrodynamics, mechanical engineering, production engineering and information technology)	applications research "science push"	basic innovation	new developments combination of known goals and new methods product innovation
existing knowledge about technical and scientific methods and solutions	knowledge and methods data base	new developments applications innovation	imitation

source: Schiele 1986

Fig. 7: Tasks and solutions in research and development

Soviet Union actually achieved its stated objective of overtaking the West by the year 1980. However, this completely overlooked the fact that the yardsticks for economic power and affluence had drastically changed in the meantime; the result is legend.

The efficiency and success of today's economies are based on creativity, innovation and flexibility, in other words primarily on human potentials and the intelligent combination of production factors, features which are now bearing fruit in the Third Industrial Revolution.

We have no ratios for measuring creativity and flexibility

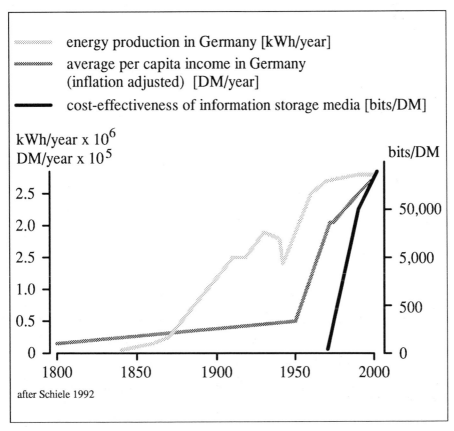

Fig. 8: Survey of industrial development

The question of factory location

Even today, agriculture supplies modern industrial society with its basic foodstuffs. It is debatable, however, to what extent a sector of the economy which only accounts for a minor and diminishing fraction of overall economic performance should be subsidized. The rules of economic logic do not always seem to apply here. Since agriculture ceased to be a major economic factor, other sectors and industries have assumed greater significance during the course of the First and Second Industrial Revolutions. This applies in particular to coal mining and steel production along with the allied industries of mechanical engineering, automobile manufacture, shipbuilding and equipment manufacture. And this industrial base is still partly supported by subsidies and structural measures, without those responsible ever asking themselves the crucial question about the suitability of these industries for the

Agriculture and the market economy do not always go hand in hand

Are agriculture, coal and steel the basis for a future economy?

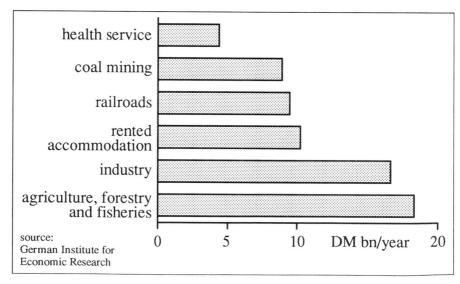

Fig. 9: The chief recipients of subsidies in Germany (1989)

future, for the time after the Third Industrial Revolution. Coal has no future as a source of energy for various reasons and the steel industry has been in a state of stagnation for years, but these facts have not led to any basic change in subsidy policies (cf. fig. 9).

In European politics and society people do not seem to be aware that other factors will be important in the 21st century; micro electronics in general and the microchip in particular, the processing and storage component for the whole of the data processing and communications industries, will be predominant. Europe has by and large missed out on the development and production of this key component, and even the USA obtains it mainly from Japan. In the Pacific we are witnessing the birth of a new economic area which will take the lead in the development, production and application of this new industrial base.

Information technology and communications form the industrial base of the 21st century

This is the field on which the battle amongst international business competitors will largely be decided. It is a trade war which Japan is cur-

> *When selecting the location for a factory or manufactory it is firstly important to ensure that the main and ancilliary materials are available, in sufficient quantities and at cheap prices, that the working wages are inexpensive and that the transport of the materials and the despatch of the goods can be achieved without great costs and danger.*

Fig. 10: Johann Beckmann on the subject of factory locations, 1796
(cf. p. 12)

We are currently losing the economic war

Have we got our priorities right?

All industrial policies must be subjected to a critical reappraisal

There is danger in misdirected subsidies unless time limits are imposed

The free market must be used to make conditions more attractive

rently winning whilst the USA and Europe are on the losing side. In the long term this will lead to the very dependencies which so much effort has been expended on avoiding in the two industries mentioned above. Since financial resources are running out, it is debatable whether we in Europe are setting the right priorities for future generations. Information and knowledge processing is a resource which is as important for the future as milk and coal.

Since we are living in a complex world which is generally beyond our control, intervention usually has undesirable consequences. This is precisely why the principles of free markets and free world trade are the natural way ahead, and why all industrial policies, including strategic ones, are to be treated with caution. The very nature of the cooperation between politics, business and science means that it concentrates for practical purposes mainly on large corporations, but since it is financed through taxation and levies, smaller companies are also affected.

So, if at all possible, subsidies - in coal mining, for example, these amount to DM 75,000 per annum for each job - should only be granted for a limited period in order to enable an industry to catch up or adjust and must then be thoroughly reconsidered. Beyond that, a subsidy may be necessary where no fair competition exists. It is the task of the state to create conditions which make its location attractive to businesses and members of society, so that it remains worthwhile for them to invest their efforts and resources there. But the state is certainly not there to make life easy for any particular enterprises or social groups.

It is well-known that Japan has developed into an economic power equal to the USA and Western Europe, in which Germany continues to play an important economic role. In addition there are other Asian countries such as Singapore, Malaysia, South Korea and Taiwan. In South America, Brazil in particular has become an exporter of industrial products. Such countries are especially likely to become dangerous competitors when low labor costs and long working hours are coupled with relatively high productivity using existing technical skills. This currently also applies in South Korea and Taiwan and, in Western Europe, to Spain and Portugal. So it would seem that anyone who wishes to always produce at the 'cheapest' location has to change sites every five years.

The Far East offers attractive markets for importers and exporters

If labor costs were the only consideration, then industry would be constantly on the move

As an industrial location, Germany offers advanced technical know-how and a high level of productivity, an excellent education system, a structure of medium-sized businesses, good transport and communications facilities com-

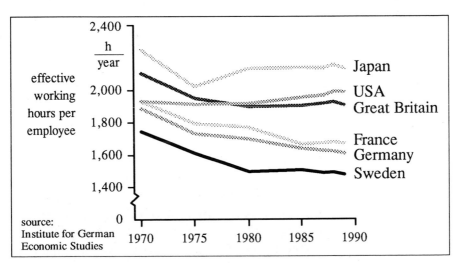

Fig. 11: International comparison of working hours

Conflicting loca-
tion factors in
Germany; are
increasing costs
affecting our
ability to innovate?

bined with political and social stability. Certain undesirable factors are, however, having a detrimental effect. The burden of taxation has reduced the funds available for investment (each new job created costs on average DM 150,000), high labor costs, shorter working week and numerous instances of government regulation and complicated application procedures (figs. 11 and 12). In the eighties, labor costs, a decisive factor in international competition, rose faster in Germany than in other industrial countries. Measured in terms of GDP, the Japanese economy has experienced considerably more growth over the last twenty years than that of Germany - over twice as much, in fact.

The international
division of labor
is the motor of
change. More
products and
manufacturing
will be lost in
future

So in the next few years even more manufacturing and products will be lost to us as the trend towards international division of labor continues. This applies especially to labor intensive products for which a significant increase in productivity can not be obtained through capital investment and automation. But this is not only true of textiles, leather goods and toys, but also applies increasingly to high-tech products. If wages in Malaysia are a tenth of those in Germany and productivity is good, then it makes good business sense to take advantage of this fact. The development, testing and production of prototypes can remain in Germany before production is shifted elsewhere within the international network. But the only companies with prospects of long-term survival are those who can design products suited to the production techniques available and finance development of both products and manufacturing processes. And in addition to product know-how, the necessary manufacturing know-how must reside

Development,
production and
market forces
demand intensive
communication

Exporting blue-
prints is not a
viable concept

within the same company. We know that in the long run it does not work to export blueprints.

Production site decisions are largely determined by the market environment. Doubtlessly, the German market is interesting from a point of view of size and its position in the center of Europe makes Germany more attractive as a manufacturing location. This is also true in the light of the efficient network of subcontractors who, because no great distances are involved, are able to meet delivery deadlines.

As a production site, Germany offers proximity to customers and suppliers

Of course Japan is a thorn in the flesh for many because of its economic strength and aggressive export policies, and of course Japan must open her markets more; and a good many of her national practices may be regarded as unacceptable trade barriers. But we must bear in mind that Japan is now the third largest importer of goods after the United States and Germany. In 1990 the average Japanese bought foreign goods to the value of US $ 1,900. An American

Japan must be developed as an import market. An emotional response is no solution

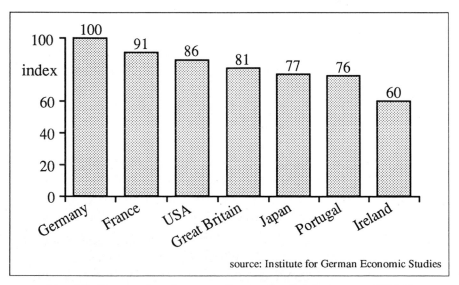

Fig. 12: International comparison of unit labor costs (1990)

In the competitive field of international specialization, relocations, winners and losers are the order of the day

by comparison spent US $ 2,050. It is wrong, as is currently happening in some quarters in the USA, to react emotionally when another country is more successful and attains supremacy in international specialization. Germany of all countries should be conscious of this, for in the fifties and sixties we, too, were 'unwelcome competitors' in Europe and the rest of the world. This confrontation between winners and losers will assume even greater proportions with the globalization of production. This is made clear by Professor Robert Reich of Harvard University in his book, 'Work of Nations':

Worldwide manufacturing chains are already a reality

"When an American buys a Pontiac Le Mans from General Motors, for example, he or she engages unwittingly in an international transaction. Of the $20,000 paid to GM, about $6,000 goes to South Korea for routine labor and assembly operations, $3,500 to Japan for advanced components (engines, transaxles, and electronics), $1,500 to West Germany for styling and design engineering, $800 to Taiwan, Singapore and Japan for small components, $500 to Britain for advertising and marketing services, and about $100 to Ireland and Barbados for data processing."[Reich 1991]

The locational debate must consider causes not symptoms

Nevertheless, the present discussion about Germany as a factory location must be taken more seriously than previous rounds of discussion. It must be borne in mind that most of the indicators used to classify competitiveness reflect the past. At best they reveal symptoms, not causes (fig. 13).

Politics and society, management and the unions are faced with the challenge of creating initial conditions that can enable Germany to retain its export-oriented industry into the 21st century. The recent example of the USA shows us that the dawn of an information and service-oriented society can only be approached successfully by retaining an efficient base of value-creating industries. Focussing on profitable business deals or service industries not only draws away important resources from production, it also distorts the long-term view of the value of the actual output of goods. We can not be warned strongly enough against changing our values along the lines of the American model - deserting the engineer for the broker.

Information and service industries need a viable manufacturing base

One increasingly important aspect in the discussion about location is the question of retaining the natural social structure, particularly in highly industrialized regions. The historical alternation between manufacturing technology

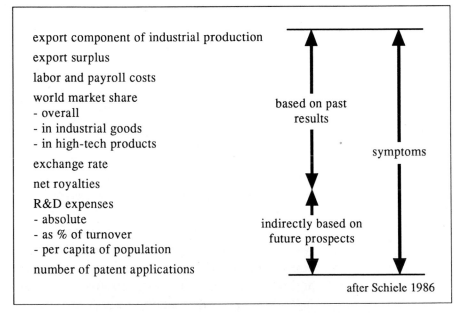

Fig. 13: Standard indicators of competitiveness

*Industry must meet
the challenge of
upholding the
natural social
structure*

and product design brought about by constantly changing demands has recently been receiving added impetus through new environmental protection requirements. This is already true for the life cycle phases of production and use. So far, the main mover here has been new legislation. As far as manufacturing is concerned, more stringent drainage regulations and laws governing protection from noxious substances and waste disposal have required certain problematic raw materials and even manufacturing processes to be dispensed with.

*The manufacture
and use of prod-
ucts must take
account of environ-
mental considera-
tions*

As far as the use of products is concerned, stricter limits or prohibitions on the use of pollutants (meaning, for example, asbestos free products, new exhaust emission standards) have had, and continue to have, an influence on product design and production techniques. As for waste disposal, schemes aimed at transferring more responsibility for disposal to manufacturers and traders are of particular importance.

*Environmental
protection is a
strong point of
Germany as a
production site*

Overall, such regulation by the authorities is seen by many as a considerable disadvantage of the location. In 1991, 1.7 percent of Germany's GDP was spent on environmental protection, two thirds of this by private industry. On the other hand there is general consensus about the fact that this policy makes sense in the long run and is indispensible. Without getting involved here in the dispute over the appropriateness of individual restrictions, we must ask if this challenge does not represent an invaluable locational advantage in the long term. Do these constraints not lead to innovations in products and processes as well as to new markets? Germany has the highest share of the world market (1990) for environmental protection technology

(21 percent), ahead of the USA (16 percent) and Japan (13 percent).

Financial estimates for solving the environmental problems inherited in the former GDR are going through the roof. A good many other countries, amongst them some of our immediate neighbors, are not yet aware of this situation, nor of its consequences. No doubt, all industrial countries will be faced with these challenges sooner or later. But then the efforts we are making today will give us an invaluable competitive edge. By that time our industry will have already adapted to the changed conditions. Furthermore, a large market for know-how and machines for environmentally safe manufacturing processes will emerge. A large number of companies have already taken up this idea as a matter of sales policy. In both capital investment and consumer goods progressively more purchasing decisions are being influenced by environmental considerations.

Environmentally safe products and manufacturing processes are a selling point

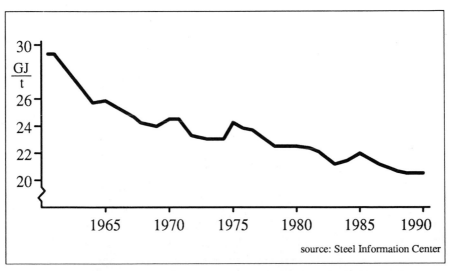

source: Steel Information Center

Fig. 14: Specific energy consumption in crude steel production

The quality of disposal must correspond to the quality of supply

The completion of material cycles will transform the waste disposal industry into a raw materials and energy industry as resources are conserved and the damage to the environment reduced. The quality of waste disposal must correspond to the quality of supply. Because the awareness of environmental issues has quite rightly been enhanced in both customers and personnel, it is essential for a factory to operate with a view to both economics and ecology. It must be both an active and a passive participant in an overall system in which resources are to be employed frugally and carefully.

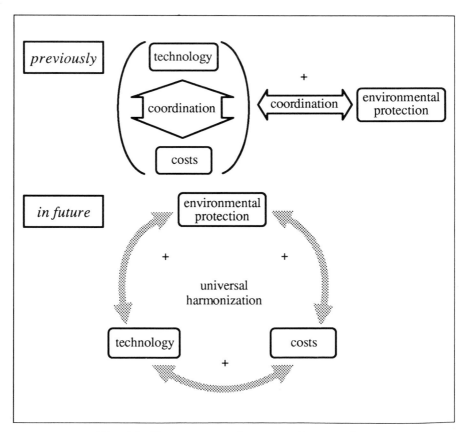

Fig. 15: Corporate environmental protection

From a commercial point of view, increased costs for environmental protection and waste disposal will - if the accounting procedures and internal information systems are correctly structured - result in decisions where economics and ecology are in harmony. The real problem lies in the short- and mid-term increase in production costs in such an area when compared with foreign locations. From the point of view of the state, or rather society, we must consider whether this might not justify restricting the import of products produced by environmentally unsafe procedures through the imposition of levies, at least for a transitional period. This would also exert a certain pressure on the conduct of foreign manufacturers. However, we must also take into account the backlash that this could have on our exports. In future, it will become a guiding principle when running a business to respect all environmental considerations in manufacturing, product consumption and waste disposal. Whereas it was once regarded as a necessary evil or as an obstacle to growth, commitment to the environment has now come to be seen as the success factor of tomorrow, even with regard to the crucial matter of staff qualifications.

When all costs are taken into account, the correct ecological decisions will follow

If all countries do not cooperate in environmental protection, then subsidies may be justified

Detailed solutions can be surprisingly simple, as the following example shows. Many processes borrowed from traditional disciplines can be an aid to finding technical and economical solutions for environmentally safe manufacturing. But we must bear in mind that these are strategies for new medium and long-term solutions.

Creativity can be borne of expediency

A domestic appliance manufacturer was not only able to use his solution to the problem of disposing waste from surface treatment to complete a perfect recycling loop in a very original way, but also killed two birds with one stone.

Environmental protection is a production factor

He replaced the oil used for the deep drawing of special steel inner chassis, which had previously had to be washed from the components prior to assembly by a laborious process, with a lubricating soap of his own invention. This soap remained on the components and could be used for the test wash operation during the final quality control stage.   [cf. Riller 1992]

Converting to water soluble paints in the automobile industry costs billions

The conversion of the spraying process to water-soluble paints which has now become necessary in the automobile industry reveals a totally different dimension. This necessitates investment in new plants costing billions and adding several hundred marks to the cost of each car. On the other hand, the damage to the environment caused by the spraying process is drastically reduced. At least for the time being, the company is in danger of encountering difficulties if the customer does not duly reward the environmentally-conscious manufacturer.

Electroplating: sealed processing chambers for integration into the manufacturing process

A final example comes from the field of electroplating, which because of the chemicals used is also a major hazard to the environment. Electroplating companies are therefore obliged to invest heavily in waste disposal, in particular for drainage filtering. This has made it more difficult to integrate the electroplating stage into the overall manufacturing process. This has led to a new approach: instead of the workpiece being transported to the individual baths for surface treatment, the 'chemical' comes - inside a sealed machine - to the workpiece. Inside the machine is a processing chamber which is filled alternately with the necessary fluids for the cleaning and separating processes. The unit manufacturer assumes the responsibility for disposal as part of the service, so that the operator is not burdened by the specific problems of an electroplating shop. He can integrate this machine into his production process and operate it as he would any other. Here, new requirements have led to new solutions and have thereby generated a forward-looking innovation.

Man and employment - aspects of sociology and ergonomics

In the sixties and seventies sociologists held the view that earning a living was losing its inherent meaning for people in industrial society. According to specialists, people regarded employment purely as a means to an end. The importance of the work content was being supplanted by a more instrumental view. Gainful employment served only to obtain material security, whilst scope for self-fulfilment was provided by increased leisure time.

It is a mistake to distinguish too clearly between work and leisure time

"As soon as man has quenched his thirst and stilled his hunger, he seeks above all happiness." This is the conclusion to which the Greek philosopher, Aristotle, had come over 2,300 years ago. Of course we must first satisfy the physical needs and requirements in order to provide a basis for other things. In the past, numerous scientists have held the view that man's various needs can be organized into a hierarchical structure. In sociology and psychology the notion advocated by the American behavioral

A traditional notion: the hierarchy of needs

scientist, Abraham H. Maslow, has received wide acceptance (fig. 17).

Attitudes towards work are changing

In the meantime a variety of objections and studies have questioned this strict hierarchy. The political, economic and technical changes of the last ten years have also left their marks on the world of work. According to sociologists, this applies especially to the attitude taken towards work. There is a trend away from material values (supplies, security) towards post-material values (social status, solidarity and self-fulfilment).

Does work make us ill, or happy?

In the year 1984 Elisabeth Noelle-Neumann and Burkhard Strümpel published the book 'Does work make us ill? Does work make us happy?' which appraised the results of surveys

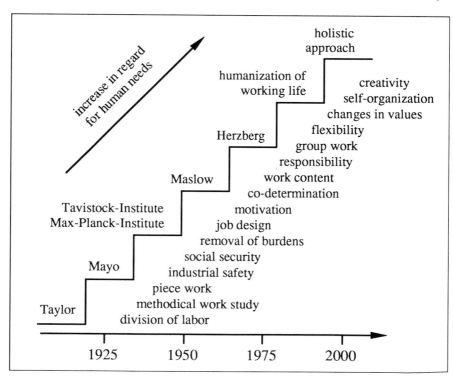

Fig. 16: Development of the social system in production

carried out in six industrial nations. This international comparison shows the Germans in a bad light. Their work ethic is poorer, their willingness to act in the best interests of their company is lower than in the other industrial nations (which included Sweden, England, the USA and Japan).

These findings are in direct contradiction of an analysis made by the Zurich social psychologist, Schmidtchen, who carried out a representative survey in the metal industry at the end of 1982. He found that leisure time had become more important for the workforce, but that work took pride of place. Most employees considered their work and their free time to be equally

Surveys in German factories reveal a positive attitude to work. In Sweden on the other hand, a study by Heinz Leymann of the University of Stockholm found that 3.5 % of workers suffer from psychological terror at work. Its removal would save DM 6 bn in lost production

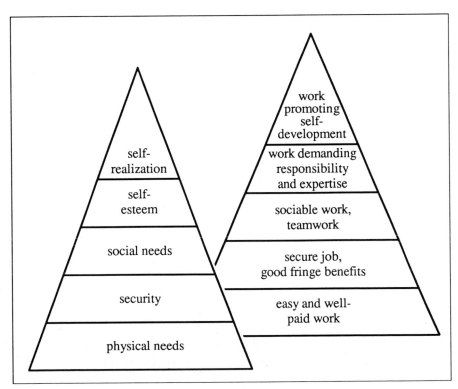

Fig. 17: Motivation pyramid according to Maslow

important. In a more recent study (January 1992), carried out by the German Institute for Applied Social Sciences (Infas) on behalf of industrial health insurance schemes, about 68 percent of West German employees questioned described their working climate as good or excellent. In particular the employees of small businesses with a payroll of ten or less expressed their satisfaction. The most important contributing factors were team spirit, independence at work and recognition by their superior. Negative aspects included intrigue, envy amongst colleagues and ill temper.

The following conclusion can be drawn from the now unsurmountable mountain of literature on the subject of changed values [Franke 1991]:

Changing values: work is a part of life

- Today's findings concerning a change in values do not give rise to a gloomy outlook for the future of working society. In spite of the great interest in increased leisure time, the importance of work as a symbol of meaningful human activity will be retained and even increased.

Financial and personal interests overlap

- However, demands placed on the nature of work are increasing. Employment is no longer seen as a means of securing an existence, but is assuming a value in its own right. The disassociation from gainful employment which has so often been observed by researchers has more to do with this change of attitudes than with a decline in morale.

- Changed organizational structures and management styles should take into account the increased desire for self-determination, individualization, participation and communication.

- The increased need for leisure time which is expressed in all the studies and the demand for the highest priority to be attached to time require a response in terms of working hours policy.

Leisure need not be an alternative to work

- There are no convincing arguments that the revaluation and expansion of leisure time has

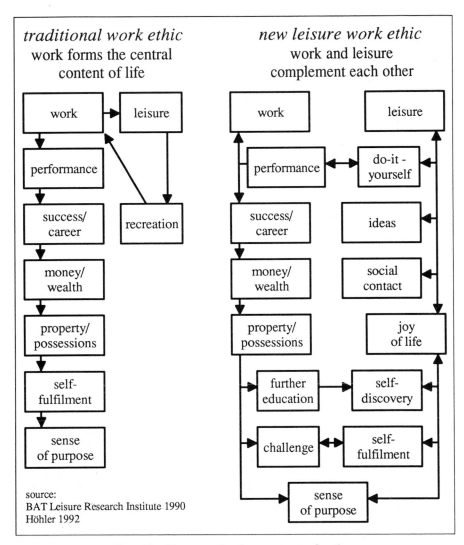

Fig. 18: Changes in the system of values

really caused it to dominate people's lives as a major and convincing alternative to gainful employment. Without the incentives, challenges, efforts, burdens and successes, but also the disappointments brought about by work, many human potentials would not be released. Man not only needs work in order to occupy his time, but also for self-development. But he also needs it as a means of communicating with his environment.

Companies must provide scope for personal fulfilment and human interaction

Today's businesses are confronted with a growth or development threshold which is determined by social change. A company must therefore be seen as a social institution. The structural nature of social relationships are reflected in corporate culture. One important design factor in corporate culture is the personal system of values of the people working within the enterprise. Three such levels of value can be identified:

level	Schneider (1970/71)	Rohmert (1972)	Hacker/Richter (1980/1986)
1	regard for limitations in human performance	performability	performability
2	avoidance of work loads injurious to health	tolerability	lack of injuriousness
3	use of reasonable pressure to increase performance	acceptability	freedom from restrictions
4	guaranteeing duties related to the level of ability	satisfaction	scope for personal development

Fig. 19: Assessment levels in human-oriented job design

- the individual's personal system of values
- the social system of values within the company
- objective cultural system of values.

Compared with the sociology of employment, ergonomics is based on a 'narrower' approach derived from the physical burden placed on the individual worker at his place of work. More modern approaches, however, strive to blend the two disciplines. The science of ergonomics therefore faces the problems we have discussed of interpreting a multicausal, multivariable process that our present knowledge scarcely equips us to quantify and which must therefore be expressed in qualitative terms.

The gap between employment sociology and ergonomics is closing

If more and more people strive for self-determination, then the necessary freedom must be created through decentralization and self-

Change must be directed to human needs

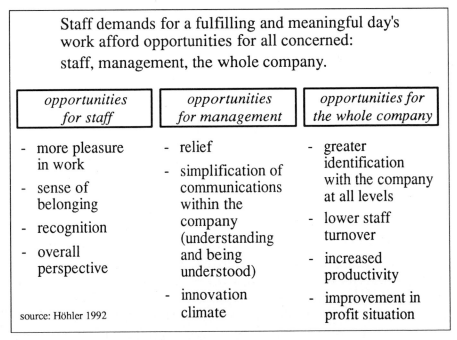

Staff demands for a fulfilling and meaningful day's work afford opportunities for all concerned: staff, management, the whole company.

opportunities for staff	*opportunities for management*	*opportunities for the whole company*
- more pleasure in work	- relief	- greater identification with the company at all levels
- sense of belonging	- simplification of communications within the company (understanding and being understood)	- lower staff turnover
- recognition		- increased productivity
- overall perspective		
source: Höhler 1992	- innovation climate	- improvement in profit situation

Fig. 20: Opportunities offered by changing values

*If all claims con-
cerning changing
values are correct,
how do we design
a factory?*

organization in order to provide scope for individual initiative for the largest possible number of employees. Seen as a creative and inventive process, paid work then becomes a means of self-fulfilment. Recognition enhances the individual's awareness of his own creativity and expands it, improving his perception of himself, his working environment and his colleagues. The result is an equal measure of educational and cultural development.

*A holistic
approach is
needed to integrate
the workforce*

Traditional forms of organization and hierarchical thinking prevent people from obtaining complete satisfaction from their work. We must therefore give them more freedom for development and involve them in project work, so that a holistic approach can be taken to improving incoming and outgoing jobs. If we see the future in intelligent manufacturing systems, we must ask where this intelligence resides. There can only be one answer: amongst the workforce, because humans are infinitely superior when it comes to the ability to combine information processing and practical action.

*The workforce's
detailed hands-on
experience must be
better exploited*

No degree of high intelligence and knowledge can substitute or compensate for the detailed experience of an employee at his place of work. So we must exploit this insight not only on the shop floor, but equally when doing business with outside suppliers. This means developing a relationship of trust which itself requires transparency and in-depth information.

*Education policy:
we must not saw
off the branch we
are sitting on*

Without wanting to get involved in a debate on education policies here, people seem to have developed a deep-seated passion for achieving the highest possible academic and vocational qualifications. There is no other way to explain the continuing flood towards our further education establishments. Whether it is necessary to rechannel this stream remains to be seen. The risks of losing one's place in the performance stakes are all too clear, whilst at the same time we can already discern a lack of qualified new staff amongst the skilled workforce. Let us once more cast our glance towards the Far East:

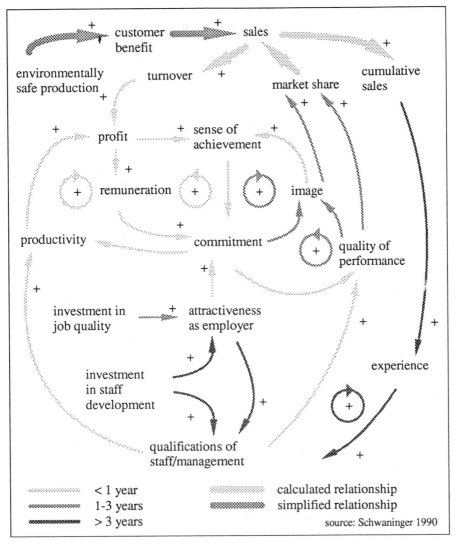

Fig. 21: Interaction of human factors

Our ability to compete in the face of adversity has its roots in the education system. We must not waste this advantage through short-sighted opportunistic reforms. It would take a long time to repair the damage

"Before lessons begin, the pupils stand in orderly rows, listen to the morning address and then march in step to their classes. The military impression is heightened by the school uniforms, which were modelled on those of the Prussian navy. Group work in class is the exception. The pupils are given prepared texts which the teacher reads through and which the pupils must reproduce as closely as possible in tests... Even industry, which should actually be satisfied (after all, don't the schools provide them with well educated, unproblematic employees?) has recognized that a rethink is required if they want to cope with the increasing pace of innovation. Independently thinking staff who are prepared to take decisions and who are not afraid of risks, who can think like entrepreneurs, are being increasingly encouraged. Moral cowards who fulfil the expectations of the examiner because they can quickly mark the correct answers without having to think about producing original solutions of their own may be brought up to work hard and to conform, but this does not give them the edge over concerns which are becoming ever more multinational in nature."   [Ederer 1991]

University education: self-development must take precedence over swotting

Could it be that the Germans of all people have the upper hand here? Instead of being so short-sighted and hankering after the standardization of education systems along the lines of international norms, we should at least bear in mind that the strength that German competitiveness has enjoyed so far is due in particular to our dual education system, our technical high schools and to a very free university system which encourages the development of the personality.

The division of labor - a feature of an efficient economy

The British economist, Adam Smith (1723-1790), used the example of pin manufacture to describe the advantages of the division of labor resulting from specialized workplaces and the success brought about through an increase in its implementation.

"The Wealth of Nations" - a classic of economic theory

"To take an example, therefore, from a very trifling manufacture; but one in which the division of labour has been very often taken notice of, the trade of the pinmaker; a workman not educated to this business (which the division of labour has rendered a distinct trade), nor acquainted with the use of the machinery employed in it (to the invention of which the same division of labour has probably given occasion), could scarce, perhaps, with his utmost industry, make one pin in a day, and certainly could not make twenty. But in the way in which this business is now carried on, not only the whole work is a peculiar trade, but it is divided into a number of branches, of which the greater part are likewise peculiar trades. One man draws out the wire, another straights it, a third cuts it, a forth points it, a fifth grinds it at the top for receiving the head...

The division of labor exploits the learning and experience curve of the specialist

And the important business of making a pin is, in this manner, divided into about eighteen distinct operations, which, in some manufactories, are all performed by distinct hands, though in others the same man will sometimes perform two or three of them. I have seen a small manufactory of this kind where ten men only were employed, and where some of them consequently performed two or three

This effect will remain valid in the future

distinct operations. But though they were very poor, and therefore but indifferently accommodated with the necessary machinery, they could, when they exerted themselves, make among them about twelve pounds of pins in a day. They are in a pound upwards of four thousand pins of a middling size. Those ten persons, therefore, could make among them upwards of forty-eight thousand pins in a day. Each person, therefore, making a tenth part of forty-eight thousand pins, might be considered as making four thousand eight hundred pins in a day."   [Smith 1776]

Specialization and simplification increase productivity even with an unskilled and semiskilled workforce

The beginning of the 20th century saw the introduction of mass production in the manufacture of consumer goods (e.g. bicycles and sewing machines). In the USA, Frederic Winslow Taylor (1856-1915) established the concept of 'scientific management'. Taylor recognized that high productivity can be achieved through staff training and the segregation of mental (planning and controlling) and physical (practical) work. Moreover, he introduced time and motion studies. The measures suggested by Taylor for the division of labor and work simplification were implemented in 1913 by Henry Ford in Detroit in the form of conveyor belt production. He compensated for its deficiencies (monotony, rapid fatigue, the stultifying of unpracticed skills and social isolation) and the resultant high staff turnover through the creation of wage incentives.

Basing production methods on the least qualified worker leads to bureaucracy and inflexibility

The work done by F.W. Taylor and Henry Ford is a very impressive example of how fruitful it can be to study the system of materials, machines, plants and production processes:

"Now, among the various methods and implements used in each element of each trade there is always one method and one implement which is quicker and better than any of the rest. And this one best method and best implement can only be discovered or developed through a scientific study and analysis of all of the methods and implements in use, together with accurate, minute, motion and time study." [Taylor 1911]

Because specialization also took place in planning, design and execution, this led to the task idea:

"The work of every workman is fully planned out by the management at least one day in advance, and each man receives in most cases complete written instructions, describing in detail the task which he is to accomplish, as well as the means to be used in doing the work." [Taylor 1911]

Time and motion studies have contributed greatly to an increase in productivity, but they have concentrated solely on process times and have ignored or excluded indirect factors

Whereas the studies of the time placed technical components in the foreground, from today's point of view the organizational aspect is dominant. The idea of a manufacturing system based on specialization was not new even in those days, but it was the first time that it had been possible to put this principle into practice consistently and on a large scale. This is Henry Ford's real achievement.

At first organization was determined by technical constraints

"I believe that this was the first moving line ever installed. The idea came in a general way from the overhead trolley that the Chicago packers use in dressing beef. We had previously assembled the fly-wheel magneto in the usual method. With one workman doing a complete job he could turn out from thirty-five to forty pieces in a nine-hour day, or about twenty minutes to an assembly. What he did alone was then spread into twenty-nine operations; that cut down the assembly time to thirteen minutes, ten seconds. Then we raised the height of the line eight inches - this was in 1914 - and cut the time to seven minutes. Further experimenting with the speed that the work should move at cut the time down to five minutes." [Ford 1922]

Productivity is the only target variable in stable mass production. Today we must also include flexibility and self-optimization

Whilst Ford was a practical man for whom all work had to be coupled with an immediate and visible improvement, Taylor laid the foundations for the discipline of production engineering with his fundamental studies in ergonomics. Taylor's system, based on the systematic investigation of processing stages and their optimized timing, was renowned in the United States as the 'one right way' of working, and it

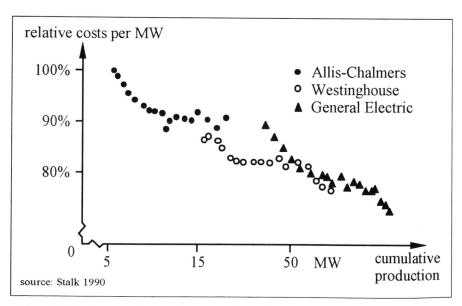

Fig. 22: Unit cost degression based on the example of steam turbines

is probably in this very generalization that the greatest error lies. Under the conditions of mass production, the productivity of an individual worker can be increased to a maximum, but job and batch production also exist, and they can be structured quite differently. Whereas productivity clearly dominated as the major factor in industrial planning until the sixties, in many areas the balance has now shifted.

Generally speaking, the discoveries and approaches of Smith and Taylor show how the familiar learning effect can be used as a basis for the organization of work. Each worker receives only as much of the content and volume of the work as is necessary to enable him to attain the shortest possible time for its execution and to maintain this level of performance. In this way he is more or less permanently programmed. It is not necessary for him to receive and slowly assimilate any new information.

In mass production both man and machine can be pre-programmed

These considerations are also valid for the division of labor within a national economy and in the international marketplace. The specialist subcontractor or supplier is always bound to be faster and better than someone who does not provide this service as his main line. In the latter case too little information is 'permanently programmed' and correspondingly more processing is required.

A specialized supplier is always better than a "jack of all trades"

Specialization therefore remains an essential component of running an efficient business. But it is not the only consideration, since other activities, such as communications and logistics, are necessary in order to provide a service, and these can reach proportions which render further specialization inadvisable.

Specialization involves increased logistics and communications work

The phases in the development of manufacturing technology can be summarized by reference to the Italian company, Beretta, which in the course of its 500-year history has undergone six important stages of restructuring (fig. 23).

Operational structuring only optimizes functions on a departmental level; no overall optimization is achieved

Operational structuring of a factory is often a hindrance to overall optimization. It is carried out only within departments and the initial conditions go unchallenged. A typical example is the ability to supply. This can be achieved through stored capacity in inventories or it can be retained in the form of machine capacity; machines wait for orders and not vice versa. If two departments are responsible, then overall optimization is not achieved, especially when optimization takes place only in terms of costs without regard for usefulness.

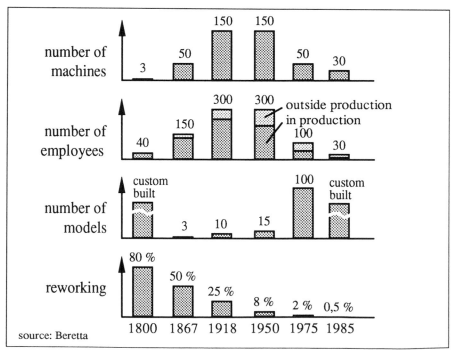

Fig. 23: Long-term structural development

This notion applies equally well to a factory's external dealings. A study of subcontractors to the automotive industry carried out by the research scientist, Susan Helper, reveals that there has been no improvement in cooperation and confidence in recent years.

"Support for this pessimistic view is provided by suppliers' perceptions of their customers' responses if one of their competitors came up with a superior component at a similar price: only 31 percent said their customer would help match the competitors' efforts (compared to 14 percent five years before). The number of customers that would switch to a rival as soon as technically feasible actually *rose* slightly, from 37 percent to 39 percent, although the difference is not statistically significant. Clearly, according to suppliers, most customers still do not perceive their supplier relationship as one that should be broken only under the most severe circumstances, after attempts to work things out have failed."   [Helper 1991]

Efficient sub-contractors and customers need mutual confidence, information and transparency

It is a two-way process

According to Eckard Jokisch, Member of the Board of Directors at Ford in Cologne, 40 percent of parts obtained from outside suppliers for the Fiesta 40 are purchased from only one source and 47 percent come from only two suppliers. The remaining suppliers become system suppliers who in turn purchase from subcontractors, whereby they must accept more responsibility. This goes for their involvement in product development and for their tie-in to production. Information and material flow must be closely coordinated with each other, which necessitates amongst other things common transport facilities.

Reducing the number of suppliers reduces the amount of logistics and communications work

Not enough atten-
tion has been paid
to interfaces

We must take into
account the whole
process chain,
including the
logistics and
transport chain

An emphasis on the advantages of specialization that we have discussed above points
towards a functional approach to factory
design. The processes involved in producing
goods are dissected and in a manner of
speaking are segregated according to type. One
advantage of this approach is that know-how
can be concentrated and a given process
completed in a shorter time. The drawback,
however, is that time and information are
wasted at each interface. With segmentation,
however, each person performs the complete
operation. For each set of products required,

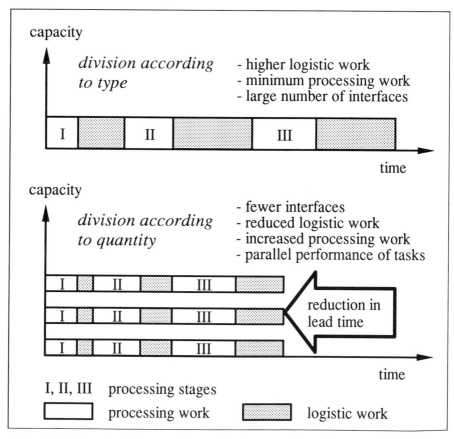

Fig. 24: Short lead time achieved by integration of processing stages

parallel identical facilities are installed. This minimizes communication and logistical work but the value-creation cycle increases because the peak of the learning curve is not reached.

Over ten years ago these considerations led to the demand for a holistic view of the process chain. Irrespective of any increase in the work content to provide human enrichment, there are also economic reasons for implementing new ideas such as group work, cellular manufactur-

Increasing the work content can often make good commercial sense

MANUFACTURING PHILOSOPHY

traditional	future-oriented

DIVISION OF LABOR

as much as possible	*as little as possible*
- simple tasks performed by the lowest possible wage groups - low labor content - large number of interfaces	- qualified work performed by the most skilled staff available - high labor content - small number of interfaces

PERFORMANCE OF WORK

- in batches - successively - delivery system/ capacity oriented	- as required - overlapping - pick-up system/ process oriented

PROCESSING TIME

- minimum for each process - maximum output per minute	- minimum for each job - maximum exploitation of each production period

MATERIAL AND INFORMATION FLOW

- regarded separately	- integrated

Fig. 25: Manufacturing philosophies

ing systems, multifunctional machine tools for total processing and even multifunctional office jobs.

Even if we still lack the financial evaluations necessary for economic or commercial optimization, it is nevertheless a useful approach for such considerations to take the overall expense to be the total costs of processing and logistics. This means striving to achieve:

$$\text{processing work} + \text{logistical work} \stackrel{!}{=} \text{minimum}$$

Traditional surcharge calculation practices result in a multiplicity of variants

Logistics is here taken in its widest sense and includes communications and control work.

This procedure also applies to the decision to introduce product variants. The traditional method of calculating surcharges often encourages a large number of variants. The more complex component or product requiring a longer processing cycle can still be the cheaper one. We must therefore take a holistic view of manufacturing processes.

According to Kaoru Ishikawa, the next person in the process chain is the customer

Would you buy the result of your own work?

One very important disadvantage of specialization is the loss of proximity to the customer. Every employee thinks and acts independently of the actual company's main aim: to create value through usefulness to the customer. This is also true of the internal relationships between employees. They must communicate with each other in order to constantly coordinate and develop demands and capacities through joint action. This is the basis of 'total quality', which has its roots in the consciousness of the workforce.

The only thing that matters is improving customer satisfaction

Why are successful businesses successful?

The prerequirements and initial conditions discussed so far establish the basis upon which manufacturing companies operate, but there is one thing which they do not necessarily create, and that is success. Success is, however, one of the keywords of business. People have been searching for the key to success for a long time, but no convincing solutions have so far been forthcoming. Most recently the hunt for success factors has resulted more and more in an inductive approach in which it is assumed that the characteristics of successful businesses can give us some indication of general design principles. The advantage of this approach lies in the practice-oriented nature of its claims. The values are based on real businesses and can therefore be verified. All the same, we should bear in mind that:

Success factors are derived inductively from successful case studies

- the selection criteria for the title 'successful business' and
- the success factors investigated

are based on subjective assessment and usually arise from observations made during consultation projects. Furthermore they are only valid for each particular situation. If this is changed, then the success factors are also affected, at least as far as their relative importance is concerned. Past success is no guarantee for the future.

Past success is no guarantee for the future

The most well-known publication based on the inductive approach is doubtlessly the one by Peters and Waterman, in which the 7-S model was worked out [Peters 1982]. This is based on the following:

- structure
- strategy
- systems
- shared values
- skills
- style
- staff

In search of excellence

If we condense and simplify this model, we can derive from it eight 'rules of thumb':

- the customer is king
- cobbler, stick to thy last
- practice is better than theory
- we just want entrepreneurs
- the workforce is the key
- we mean what we say, and we act accordingly
- cut red tape
- as much management as necessary, as little control as possible

or

Strategic and operative approaches are two different matters

- We perform services: strategic approach.
- We are the subject of constant regeneration: operative approach.

The latter can be put into practice in the short term - one to three years - and above all it helps us to get away from the critical break-even point, whilst the first is more drawn-out, requiring as a rule from five to ten years.

But the fact that these principles are no guarantee of long-term success is shown by the following example, listed amongst the 'success stories':

"At IBM, management adheres strictly to the rule of the three-year staff rotation. Few staff jobs are manned by 'career staffers'; they are manned by line officers. Moreover, those who do get into the rotation on the corporate staff know that within three years they are going back out of the line again. It is a marvelous check on the invention of complex systems. If you know you are going to become a user within thirty-six months, you are not likely to invent an overbearing bureaucracy during your brief sojourn on the other side of the fence."   [Peters 1982]

There are examples which contradict these principles

Line personnel are employed in staff cells

In the mid-eighties IBM underwent major restructuring with the goal of becoming more customer-oriented and in recent times the need for still further action has become evident:

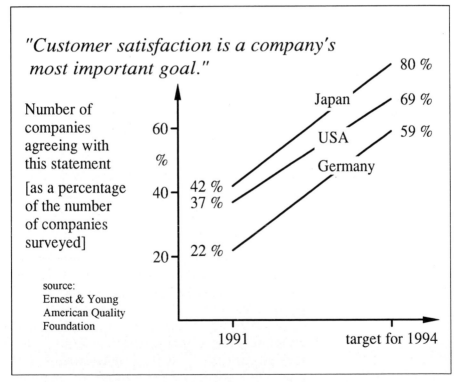

Fig. 26: Customer benefit as a success factor

Can a cumbersome elephant be transformed into a fleet-footed gazelle?

"An elephant is certainly not as sprightly as a gazelle, says Hans-Olaf Henkel, head of IBM Germany. The elephant - by this Henkel is referring to his own company. The goal that IBM has set itself for 1992 is, however, no less than the task of making a fleet-footed gazelle out of a cumbersome elephant. The world's largest computer company with its headquarters in Armonk in New York State has prescribed radical reforms for itself - in addition to drastic cost-cutting exercises and staff reductions involving about 20,000 job losses. Above all a thorough reorganization is planned in order to solve the company's 'home-made problem', which Henkel includes among the reasons why the computer giant has hit difficulties and is experiencing stagnating sales, decreasing profits and considerable loss of market shares..."

[Blick durch die Wirtschaft, Jan 22, 1992]

The whole problem of the inductive approach is illuminated by an ex-post examination of the corporate development of firms which were once considered highly successful:

It is not easy to march forward whilst looking back

"After 48 years of profitable operation, Caterpillar made the mistake of believing in its own forecasts. In 1975 the thinking at Cat was that 'the infrastructure of the world is falling apart, therefore more bridges, more dams, more construction will be necessary.' Caterpillar thereupon began to invest two billion dollars in new capacities. From a logical point of view this was correct. But the world said: 'let the infrastructure fall apart. We don't have the money.' The market for heavy construction machinery fell by thirty percent..."

[Kami 1988]

McKinsey, in collaboration with Professor H. Schulz of the Technical University in Darmstadt, has investigated the particular circumstances of the German mechanical engineering giants [Schulz 1991].

To sum up the basic findings of these studies, we can conclude that there is no patent recipe for corporate success. What we *can* do is identify a number of strategies which can be regarded in various ways as 'levers' to success:

A study of mechanical engineering firms identifies "levers" to success

- The complexity of the product range tends to be low. Concentration on a small number of products and important customers produces a simple - today one would say 'lean' - system.

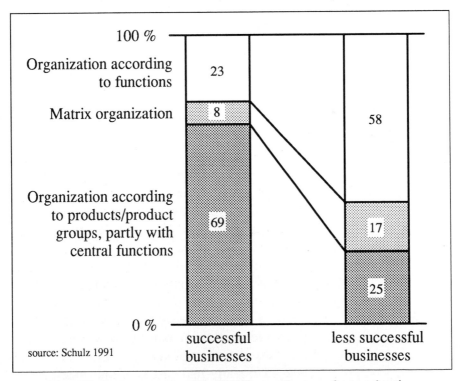

Fig. 27: Success potential of different forms of organization
(results of a study)

- Vertical range of manufacture is reduced through concentrating on operative strengths. At the same time, contacts to suppliers are improved.

- Location and logistics are in keeping with the product and the market.

- Product development is based on the rapid implementation of minor innovations and detailed collaboration with the customer.

- The use of computerized techniques is a considerable aid to reducing manufacturing costs and throughput times and brings an improvement in quality.

- Finally, the organization is characterized by a simple, decentralized structure with a high degree of training in all areas. Central functions are partly allocated to product groups.

An external enemy is important

The concept of an external enemy also seems to contribute significantly to success. The company's resources are then not wasted on internal conflict. So all employees must be aware of the competitive situation and the objectives and measures to be derived from it.

There are many reasons for success

We have seen time and time again how quickly successful businesses can lose their position when external circumstances change. This is a warning to all those who seek handy methods which will guarantee success, and it confirms the suspicions of all those who have always felt that reality is a much more complex matter. Success can indeed be measured, but its roots are to be found in the intricate interrelationships of a large number of non-linear factors. In the end, they defy comprehension and can not be reduced to ready-made rules of management.

The results of such studies should not therefore be taken as guidelines but as building blocks in the search for answers to the question of corporate success. Of course, in many specific cases it is possible to recommend certain basic strategies, for example with regard to the competitive situation (fig. 28). But even then we are still only looking at the past.

There are only guidelines, no ready-made methods

One positive example is the Fisons company in Great Britain. It had made its name as a major manufacturer of fertilizers. This had led to activities in the fields of measuring instruments and pharmaceutical products. When profits started to decrease, Fisons had a study made in order to develop strategies for the future. The highly regarded firm of market consultants came to the conclusion that they should concentrate on the core area of fertilizers once again. The company said, "the study is very good, but we don't like the conclusions." They sold the core business at a

A case study: Fisons in Great Britain

One principle is to concentrate on the core business, but does the core business have a future?

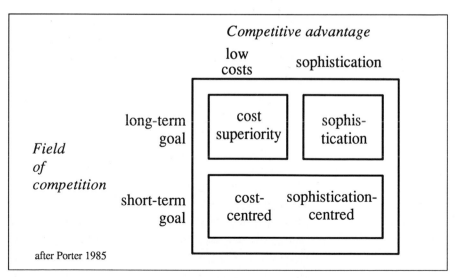

Fig. 28: Competitive strategies

Rapid innovation through small, autonomous production units

good price and used the capital to acquire smaller companies all over the world with innovative capacity in the field of scientific measuring equipment for analytical studies. Today Fisons Instruments employs about 3,500 staff and the turnover amounts to DM 900 million, but the philosophy is still the same: 'small is beautiful'. They maintain a relatively large number of small, autonomous production facilities with a team of managers, developers and production specialists. This is the reason for the constantly new, excellent and innovative products with which they can react quickly to customer requirements.

The question which is constantly being raised about how to implement and integrate such insights into a single vision has led to the development of new approaches to organizational design throughout the world.

Outlines of some approaches from the USA and Japan

The global search for visions

All over the world experts are doing their utmost to find *one* formula that will bring corporate success. This has given rise to numerous visionary and practical approaches and it is not the purpose of this study to compile a collection of possibilities that have already been postulated. We will therefore restrict ourselves to a small number of particularly promising approaches and we can only give a brief outline even of these. In the main our attention will be centered - obviously, some readers might say - on what are taken to be the major competitors in the global marketplace, the USA and Japan. This is all the more justified because the intensive research is being carried out in the relevant subjects in these countries, no less so than it is here. Without advocating a return to the age of pilgrimages overseas or to the Far East, it can do no harm to cast a glance in that direction.

American industry has always regarded the world market differently to, for example, the Europeans. This is understandable in view of the vastness of the domestic market, in which such problems as differing standards, customs barriers and legal and political instabilities were and are largely unknown. The tendency to concentrate on this market in difficult times can still be observed today. And government-level agreements with Japan on foreign trade reinforce this impression still further.

American industry is concentrating on its domestic market

Nevertheless, there are more and more voices warning against such a disastrous trend. In a self-critical analysis, John Young, president of Hewlett Packard, lists five myths which are still being propagated to give the Americans a feeling of technical superiority [Manufacturing Engineering 1992]:

Myth 1: The leading edge lost in some older industries is perceived to be compensated for by superiority in forward-looking areas requiring intensive know-how.

Many Americans still hang on to the myth of technical leadership

Since the mid-eighties, however, the balance has been shifting to the detriment of the Americans. This trend is revealed by the trade deficit in high-tech areas which has persisted since 1986.

Myth 2: The trend referred to above is due to the concentration on state-of-the-art technology in the respective field of application. The mass market for consumer electronics, for example, is still open to competition.

This assessment can hardly be sustained. It is precisely in key technologies such as in the manufacture of integrated circuits and optical storage chips that American suppliers no longer dominate.

The 5 myths of American self-assessment in industry

Myth 3: Far Eastern competitors in particular are reputed to be guilty of merely copying technical solutions and are therefore only 'jumping on the technological bandwagon'.

This was certainly true for a long time, but is now definitely a thing of the past. Nowadays, 48 percent of patent applications filed in the United States are by foreign inventors.

Myth 4: The list of Nobel Prize winners continues to indicate America's leading role in fundamental areas of research.

Incorrect self-assessment can have disastrous consequences

However, little attention is paid to the conversion of these achievements into marketable products.

Myth 5: The reaction to the 'Sputnik shock' in 1957, namely the space program which resulted in success in the sixties, demonstrates the ability to channel all available energy into meeting an open challenge.

Such a confrontation, however, is being cleverly averted by the Japanese competition. A precautionary and partial retreat (e.g. in the question of Japanese automobile exports) goes hand-in-hand with concentrated attacks in a number of significant areas which attract less publicity. The war of attrition fought in the market for semiconductors, for example, has been won by Japan almost without a murmur.

In addition to demanding a change of awareness in the areas mentioned above, a panel of American management experts has compiled a list of the characteristics of the successful company of the future. They advocate the 'agile company', the three essential features of which are constant change, rapid response and an extended notion of quality.

The "agile company" is advocated

Constant change:
A competitive advantage is no longer measured in years and months, but in weeks. This means that the whole manufacturing system can not even attain a state of stability, but must constantly be adapted to changing circumstances. Managing production therefore means managing change. Hierarchically structured organizations which have been stable for many years are hardly in a position to bring about such change. According to the experts in the panel, five basic elements are required for the continuous regeneration of a company:

Established hierarchical organizations tend to be lethargic

- a long-term vision
- routes which lead there
- a comparison between the resources required and those available
- a strategic plan for their development
- a far-reaching program of staff training.

Rapid speed of response:
The ability to respond with maximum speed can only be achieved through intensive cooperation, both inside and outside the company. But without a large measure of confidence in the abilities and reliability of one's partners, this kind of collaboration can not develop. There must be an end to information monopolies, a matter which poses questions for the entire business culture. Ed Miller, President of the 'National Center for

Speed of response should be improved still further through computer integration

Marketing Sciences', is working on the vision of a worldwide communication network. With this network, any version of any product can be put into production at any location without delay. This idea applies the principle of computer integrated manufacturing on a global scale. Eight such networked manufacturing sites are operating in the USA as part of a pilot scheme.

Extended notion of quality:
The quality of a product is not restricted to its freedom from defects. The product is only the material basis of a customer-supplier relationship. In future, justice must be done to all aspects of this relationship through extending the notion of quality. American consumers are no longer as ready as they were to accept price reductions as compensation for poor quality. This is in line with a development which took place in Germany some years ago.

Quality does not end at the product

The main framework conditions for these three success factors are provided by human relations and government policy:

Human relations:
In this regard, the experts take their model from the Far East. The creation of a motivating working environment, long-term employment, co-determination and shared decision making at all levels and the abolition of the straitjacket of rules and directives are conducive to a more performance-oriented 'we' mentality.

"Hiring and firing" does no-one any good, least of all the company

A survey of 300 companies in the Midwest came to the definite conclusion that virtually all target variables, such as market shares and product quality, can best be attained through strategies which influence the social system. Engineering and technology play a much less significant role.

The role of government:
The American experts complain that subsidies
for the manufacturing industries are inadequate
because the government only thinks and acts
according to short-term considerations. This is
evident in research policy deficits, inadequacies
in the creation of a modern infrastructure, and
poor conditions on the money markets, but
above all in years of neglect of the education
system. It is precisely the latter aspect which is
a sore point in the social structure of the United
States. It should be noted here that in the USA
the role of the state in business life has always
been a controversial matter, resulting in quite
conflicting views.

*The role of the
American govern-
ment comes under
critical scrutiny*

Peter F. Drucker envisages the implementation
of four basic principles in the 'postmodern
factory' of the year 1999 [Drucker 1990]:

- statistical quality control
- new manufacturing accounting
- 'flotilla' organization
- systems design

*Drucker formu-
lates four princi-
ples for the "post-
modern factory"*

In its original sense the concept of statistical
quality control, first developed in the USA but
largely ignored there for a long time, concerns
itself with the manufacturing *process*. However,
the quality of goods and services must go way
beyond the mere regulation of process variables. Once again, human factors are of particular importance. By concentrating on the value-
creating and therefore crucial processes, total
quality is achieved with the minimum input of
resources. According to Drucker this brings
about a harmonization of the two schools of
thought, 'scientific management' and 'human
resources'.

Total quality

Real cost analysis

The value of accounting systems based on direct labor costs is debatable if these costs only constitute a minor proportion of the total costs. In many cases labor costs are below 20 percent, but continue to serve as the basis of calculation for costs going far beyond this, but which can not be correctly allocated. Investment decisions are usually based exclusively on variables which can be determined directly. Traditional accounting methods draw their data from the effective production of parts and therefore ignore the effects of down time and scrap. What is more, costing systems do not take into account the questions of customer-oriented manufacture, such as the acceptance of standardized products. Put bluntly:

Down time and scrap are ignored

"Hardly any product improvement, let alone an innovation, can be justified by traditional methods of cost-analysis."   [Drucker 1990]

"Time" can be the main reference variable for decision making

Time is therefore proposed as a unit of measurement for a new cost accounting model. The use of time, whether for the manufacture of goods (or even scrap) or for the storage of parts, is linked to a fixed cost factor. So in this system all activities are designed to minimize the use of time.

In Drucker's view the problem of evaluating unquantifiable variables (such as the effects of automation on the market share) has yet to be solved. Even if these relationships can not be integrated into the costing system of the future, they will still form an important basis for executive decisions.

A factory must not be a "battleship"

Drucker compares today's factories with a cumbersome 'battleship' navigating in adverse conditions. The postmodern factory on the other hand is likened more to a flotilla, consisting of modules which complement each other whilst moving in the same direction. Applied to manufacturing, such a module could be a stage in the manufacturing process.

"And each, like the ships in a flotilla, will be maneuverable, both in terms of its position in the entire process and its relationship to other modules."

Modular organization - like a flotilla

Such a modular organization is not only more flexible in operation, but can also allow rapid changes in design in response to changed demands. Drucker also develops an interesting vision for the flow of information, which we shall come back to later:

"In the factory of 1999, sectors and departments will have to think through what information they owe to whom and what information they need from whom. A good deal of this information will flow sideways and across department lines, not upstairs. The factory of 1999 will be an information network. Consequently, all the managers in a plant will have to know and understand the entire process... Managers will have to think and act as team members, mindful of the performance of the whole. Above all, they will have to ask: What do the people running the other modules need to know about the characteristics, the capacity, the plans, and the performance of my unit? And what, in turn, do we in my module need to know about theirs?"

The factory as an information network with horizontal communication between modules

In the case of customer-oriented production, manufacturing itself is only one component in

*Production is
overvalued when
compared to
service*

the process of providing goods and services. The traditional way of looking at things often overvalues this component and fails to give due attention to other areas such as after-sales service. If Caterpillar can supply any spare part to any place in the world, then this has major consequences for the whole company. This means that the latter must be treated as a system to be coordinated and directed as a complete unit. On the other hand a conscious marketing decision can have the opposite effect. For example, Honda established an independent network of dealers in the USA to market their Acura model.

*Global information
and production
networks should be
built*

To sum up, from an American point of view it is necessary, in addition to solving 'home made' problems, to establish and operate nationwide information and manufacturing networks. Adaptability, total quality, but in particular the inclusion of employees on all levels, are elements of future manufacturing structures. Furthermore, emphasis is placed on the inadequacies of existing evaluation factors and a new concept for cooperation amongst all divisions is called for.

*In Japan, lean
production is still
being developed*

In Japan, too, there is increasingly widespread acceptance of the need to secure long-term competitiveness by means of really new approaches [Engel 1990]. This is even more astonishing since companies in many parts of the West are striving to imitate the putative vision of lean production. The very fact that people in Japan are obviously not satisfied with this level of technology should give advocates of imitative strategies food for thought.

*Anyone can buy
automation*

If all efforts are concentrated on computer aided and automated value creating processes, a factory can be 'exported', but would have to tramp gypsy-fashion through numerous countries in succession. In the Far East, for example, this would mean Korea, Malaysia and so on.

Ironically, the vision of a 'CIM factory' has shunted itself to the sidelines. The increased significance being attached to time as a production factor is transforming manufacturing increasingly from a static into a dynamic system. But such an environment brings out even more weaknesses in computer aided systems. According to Norio Okino (University of Kyoto), the following deficiencies and fallacies can be identified:

Highly dynamical systems reveal the weaknesses of computer-controlled processes

- exaggerated confidence in the abilities of computers
- excessive faith in mathematical optimization processes
- lack of diagnostic certainty
- manufacturing operations are not adequately reproduced
- automated processes do not sufficiently exploit human talents

The greatest problem area is found to be in central planning and control.

Working from the model of biological organisms, a Japanese study group has conceived the vision of a 'bionic manufacturing system', in which three essential properties of the natural model are realized:

Japan: the bionic manufacturing system

- spontaneity
- mobility
- harmony

To the advocates of the bionic approach four characteristics of biological organisms seem to be particularly worthy of imitation:

- the integration of functional elements and hierarchies
- the arrangement of information on DNA*
- the use of natural intelligence
- dynamic structure and social harmony.

The storage and processing of information characterize the system

In particular, claims about bionic manufacturing accord a great deal of importance to the idea of a DNA-type information system. The main question here is how much and which information it is necessary to store in the manufacturing system. This information should be 'inherited', i.e. passed on in encoded form. This is supposed to ensure that the intelligence needed for production is permanently available. All information which is not based on DNA, on the other hand, comes from intuitive intelligence and must therefore be stored in a retrieval system of a different nature. This should have features analogous to the brain.

Organizations are organisms which interact in networks

Simulation must correspond to real operation

This approach goes so far as to dispense completely with central planning and administration. The autonomous units are connected to each other entirely by a comprehensive information system which makes all information available everywhere throughout the system. Dialog takes place in the form of an enquiry to which each other element can react spontaneously. Such a system offers two operating modes: simulation and real operation, making it possible to examine the (barely predictable) consequences of individual decisions.

Neural networks and fuzzy logic appear to be suitable instruments for computer links because of their proximity to biological models. Moreover, hierarchical object classes ('modelons')

---

* **deoxyribon**ucleic **acid**, carrier of genetic information

are defined, with which it is possible to structure the bionic factory. The strict hierarchy which this involves is favored here because it conforms to the Japanese social model. The originators themselves are critical of the fact that this leads back to a hierarchical communication structure, which is precisely what they wanted to avoid.

Even the bionic factory retains a hierarchy

Furthermore, it is justified at this point to ask whether a factory without central direction might not quickly degenerate into a conglomerate of elements, each pursuing their own interests and therefore developing in different directions. No methods of rationalization involving the amalgamation of identical functions can be taken advantage of. Yusaku Shibata, the head of a private research institute, explicitly demands the total decentralization of all planning activities.

The duplication of identical functions must be accepted

In 1990 a program called 'Intelligent Manufacturing Systems' (IMS) was launched by MITI in order to tackle a variety of shortcomings in industrial manufacturing. The goal is to encourage worldwide cooperation, specifically with the United States and the European Community. Canada and Australia have since been included in a two-year feasibility study started in 1992. The controlled transfer of knowledge, new manufacturing techniques and their systematization and standardization should form the basis for the 'intelligent manufacturing systems' of the 21st century. MITI defines an *intelligent manufacturing system* as:

MITI has launched an initiative for international research cooperation - IMS

A feasibility study is currently in progress

"a system for improving productivity through

- systematization of all the abstract elements involved in manufacturing

> - flexible integration of the whole range of activities throughout the company (from order entry through development and manufacturing to sales), characterized by the promotion of optimum interaction between humans and intelligent machines."

As conceived by its creators, the program is restricted to the industrial regions indicated, which lends it a regulatory dimension since newly industrialized countries do not participate. Furthermore, it is assumed that the participants are engaged in the development or production of different lines and that competitive conflicts therefore do not arise. The elements of an 'intelligent manufacturing system' from a Japanese point of view are:

- universally applicable
- autodidactic and adaptable
- thoroughly networked with information systems with open interfaces
- expandable.

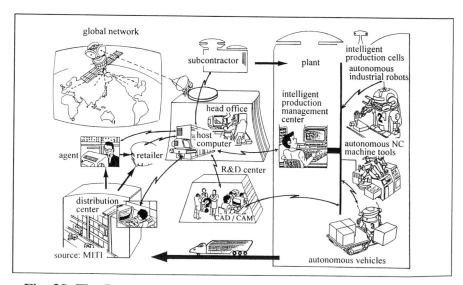

Fig. 29: The Japanese vision of an intelligent manufacturing system

When we contrast this to the concept of 'bionic manufacturing', it becomes clear how heavily the program depends on technology. So even in the Far East the debate about strategy is a controversial one. It is interesting that the vision exists of developing some kind of 'ultimate' - and even universally adoptable - manufacturing system for the 21st century. The existence or feasibility of such a system is doubtful.

In Japan an ultimate manufacturing system is envisaged for the 21st century

topic	integration/ systematization of existing technology	standardization	next-generation technology
basic principles of system design		harmonious systems; open systems	cooperative systems; modular systems; free topology systems
methods of constructing adaptive systems			holonic, open, autonomous, modular, community-oriented, self-organizing manufacturing
support technology for system design	system construction tools; modeling, database (processing database); simulation (engineering, manufacturing)	information transformation standardization; cell standardization; public database	*intelligent* manufacturing systems, synthetic modeling, manufacturing platforms, information processing; factory modeling; function-driven product modeling; engineering factories
system management; evaluation technology	intelligent decentralized controllers	evaluation of manufacturing systems; QA; decentralized controllers	dynamic distributed processing; autonomous rearrangement; knowledge base

Fig. 30: System design and configuration methods in the IMS project

*Creative imple-
mentation is more
successful than
mistrust*

The resonance in the West, in particular in industrial circles, has been somewhat reserved, for one reason because of the fear of the information flowing only in one direction. Whether such phalanx-type thinking is appropriate to our times and whether it can be sustained is, however, rather doubtful. After all, it is absolutely vital for us to understand how other countries think and act. But then we must have the creativity to draw our own conclusions, develop the appropriate measures and act accordingly.

topic	integration/ systemization of existing technology	standardization	next-generation technology
processing cells/ processing technology	precision assurance technology; multifunction processing technology	flexible tooling; processing data base	ASIC-based controllers for factory automation; autonomous decentralized intelligent processing cells; new-material tools; innovative processing technology
assembly cells/ robots	high-robustness, high-precision robots	flexible handling	autonomous robots; multi-function assembly equipment
sensors/ measurement cells	advanced sensors; online measurement/inspection	3-dimensional shape inspection system	AI-supported sensors fusion; multifunction inspection systems
automated transportation/ warehousing	advanced AGV	modular rack-type warehouses	autonomous AGV/ automated warehouses
controllers			intelligent decentralized controllers

Fig. 31: System components and process technology (IMS project)

Cultural consequences are more serious than technical consequences

Before we proceed to the actual subject of our deliberations - concerning a new paradigm - we should first cast a glance at the possible consequences of such a radical transformation. Philosophical, ideological and sociological consequences - here grouped together under the heading 'cultural consequences' - have a much more drastic effect overall and have, as history teaches us, a much greater impact than the effects of science and technology. It is after all a matter of integrating technology and society across disciplinary borders, or rather reintegrating them, since the drifting apart of the 'two cultures' is a hallmark of today's modern techno-scientific civilization. The aim is to reunite the two worlds of culture/art and science/technology. Segregating them into science and everyday life, into education and training, has been disastrous.

Segregating culture and technology would be disastrous for us

Engineers do not need supervisors, but partners in dialog - starting with training

It is very one-sided to demand an appraisal and institutionalization of the consequences of technological developments but at the same time to deny the existence of any cultural impact. The two are closely interrelated. It will provide a more ethical educational basis for an engineer's activities if the intelligentsia in turn concern themselves seriously with the impact of technology and thereby contribute effectively to the debate. This will provide for communication between the two worlds even during training. The present increase in demand for non-technical subjects in engineering courses must not be seen as a purely supplemental component of technical training but must be fully integrated into courses.

Non-technical courses must not be regarded as merely supplementary

China had the lead in technology until the late Middle Ages

The ancient cultures of Egypt and Greece achieved great feats of science and technology, but initially this tradition did not persist into the Roman Empire and the Christian West. There are numerous examples of the suppression of scientific knowledge during this period. In the Middle Ages China seems to have been ahead in matters of science. However, differences in culture and patterns of thinking virtually precluded the transfer of knowledge, although this was easier with purely technical solutions. Of course there were parallel inventions, but a

from China to the West:	time difference in centuries
smallpox vaccination	1-7
crossbow	13
depth drilling	11
cast iron	10-12
gimbal mount	8-9
clock escapement	6
segmental arch bridge	7
canal locks	7-17
nautical construction principles	>10
gunpowder	4
magnetic compass	11
paper	12
printing press (with movable type)	4
porcelain	11-13
from the West to China	time difference in centuries
screw	14
power pump for fluids	18
crankshaft	3

source:
Needham 1978

Fig. 32: Exchange of technical solutions between East and West

considerable transfer of technology did take place, with most of the inventions coming from China (fig. 32).

This took place within the cultural environment of Tang Taoism and Sung Neoconfucianism. 'Tao' is the structure of all things, which is complemented by 'Li', the fine structure of individual natural objects. Matter can create consciousness once it has attained a sufficiently high degree of structure and organization. This philosophy could have brought about a break-through in Chinese science if mathematics had been developed and incorporated into these theories. But this never happened and a purely humanistic doctrine took over. So it was in the West that the foundations for the global dominance of European science and technology were laid down in the form of mathematical formulae by Galileo, Descartes and Newton. Leibniz tried (under the influence of Chinese philosophy) to overcome the contradiction between the idealism of theology and the materialism of this new science, but in the end, this goal eluded him.

The technological superiority of the West was based on analytical thinking and the development of mathematics

Today it is more apparent than ever before that we must revise our view of the world. In the science of manufacturing in particular, Asian cultures are currently achieving partly better results more quickly. Their cultural and historical background seems to enable them, at least under the present conditions, to attain a superior interplay between man, technology and organization. Although it is still in its early days, the history of industry is laden with examples of structural change. Technologies, professions and whole industries come and go. The process is irresistable; past experience shows that it is folly to expend one's energies in an attempt to

The successful ideologies and practices of the past 300 years are outliving their usefulness

*We must modify
our view of the
world*

stem the tide. A competitive German industry in the 21st century is certain to be different to that of today, but any approaches worthy of development must be in keeping with our cultural heritage. We shall proceed to discuss which approaches should be adopted.

3. Organizational Design - a Key Component of Strategy

A fundamental requirement for a company aiming for long-term success in a complex theatre of operations is a suitable strategy. In keeping with its martial origin, strategy, originally a term for the art of military leadership, can be applied to business life to denote the application of rules with the prime objective of increasing the probability of a desired result. This usually means ensuring the long-term survival of the organization. Determining which correct and well-informed decisions are to be taken is the object of strategic planning, for which four basic functions can be identified:

Strategy: increasing the likelihood of achieving a specific objective

The *performance function* aims to ensure a greater degree of goal attainment and a more efficient use of human effort or of scarce resources. The *innovation function* is concerned with changes in thought content, behavior patterns or things. The coordination of materially and chronologically interdependent individual decisions takes place within the framework of the *coordination function.* Finally, the *motivation function* is concerned with obtaining the consensus of all participants on the contents of planning.

Various organizational and executive functions ensure the survival of an enterprise

All planning functions are designed to achieve the above-mentioned basic goal of ensuring survival. From this, partial goals may in turn be derived in order to maintain profitability, defend against competition and maintain the innovative potential needed for survival. At the present time more than ever before, strategy means bringing about far-reaching changes in all vital organs of an enterprise: corporate culture must

Strategy today: a revolution in corporate culture

be revolutionized. Of course it is a fundamental aim of any company to show a profit; this is as true today as it always was. But this alone can not be the maxim of a successful business ideology. The fact that it has taken root within a given social environment is an expression of the prevalent philosophy or social culture and every corporate philosophy and culture should be treated as a subset thereof. This is the only way to ensure long-term success consistency.

In a changing environment a company is a subset which is subject to influences

From this it follows that factories can not simply be transplanted into a foreign cultural environment. I see here no contradiction to the reports about Japanese companies which structure and manage their European factories along the lines of Far Eastern models. Either they exploit virtues which are also present, although perhaps hitherto undiscovered and unused, in the western hemisphere, or they rely on psychological pressure, which will be avenged in the long term. It is no secret that the transplants in Great Britain are ruled with an iron fist - starting with the hiring of the workforce. This concept surely can not be tenable in the long term. Rather - to use a metaphor - the pendulum is swinging in the other direction after longstanding problems could not be overcome.

A company's culture must correspond to its social environment

The production manager of a German consumer electronics factory operating under Far Eastern leadership reports that he has dropped the idea of a quality control circle in its original form outside working hours, and provides the following explanation: in the parent company a large number of workers live far from their families, and since they are accommodated in hostels, quality control circles are formed spontaneously in leisure time as a kind of by-product. The borderline between work and leisure time has become somewhat hazy.

We have already observed in a different context that a demystification of foreign cultural circles is necessary. This will direct our attention to what we must do, namely concentrate on our own environment and exploit the potential hidden within it. In order to benefit from these resources we must have knowledge of them. As banal as this assertion may seem, it is difficult to tie down cultural environmental factors. And here we can hardly avoid taking a look at the intellectual and scientific history of the West. The main reason for investigating cultural aspects is to find optimum corporate structures resting on a solid foundation - a decisive strategic potential.

We must concentrate on our own strengths and direct our energies towards utilizing them

In order to come to terms with the organizational aspects of a structure as complex as a manufacturing enterprise, we usually construct a model of the conditions and processes involved. And in this very first step mistakes can be made which call the value of the whole exercise into question. First of all, the model may be designed from 'above' or from outside, that is, it is originated by persons whose detailed knowledge of the processes and conditions is generally fairly limited. The model therefore represents an image of something that has been preconceived as the ideal structure. It should not surprise us, therefore, if those solutions which were already preferred are found to be ideal, even when computer aided methods such as simulations are used. A model designed on the lines of the existing or typical organizational structure of a company can not lead us to solutions which question this very

Many company models no longer bear comparison with reality

In organizational design we often use traditional models and notions. This is not the way to achieve optimization

organization itself: a typical example of a self-fulfilling prophecy.

The design frame-work is often too coarse

Furthermore, a very coarse framework is often used during the modelling process, because this requires less effort. The system elements themselves are complex structures, but they are often delineated according to traditional notions requiring a high degree of simplification. So no amount of subsequent processing can produce solutions with a structure finer than that of the smallest system elements represented.

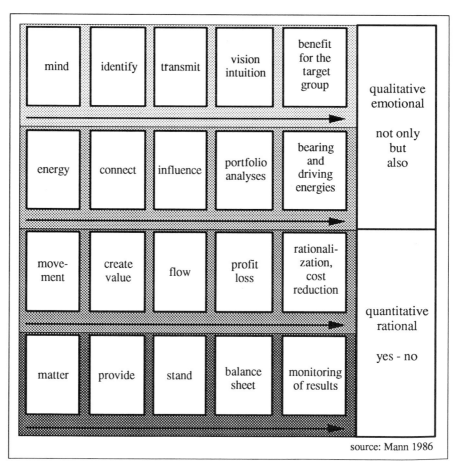

mind	identify	transmit	vision intuition	benefit for the target group	qualitative emotional
energy	connect	influence	portfolio analyses	bearing and driving energies	not only but also
move-ment	create value	flow	profit loss	rationali-zation, cost reduction	quantitative rational
matter	provide	stand	balance sheet	monitoring of results	yes - no

source: Mann 1986

Fig. 33: Corporate model: four levels of observation

A deficiency no less far-reaching in the design of models lies in the formulation of the relationships between the system elements and the identification of control parameters. This notion is best illustrated by an example:

In many companies the output of the workforce is regulated by means of performance quotas, normally in terms of time per unit of performance. This parameter therefore only influences quantity. Other goals such as quality are unaffected. The logical consequence of this is a less than optimum overall production. As illogical as it sounds, this situation is still the rule rather than the exception. More than ten percent of assembly work in German automobile factories is devoted to the correction of defects [Womack 1990]. In some cases, the enforced flow of mass production assembly work leads to defective parts deliberately being used. Rigid control mechanisms do not permit any alternative. From a point of view of system theory, we are faced with a crass example of incorrect regulating parameters; the control variables selected are quite unsuited to the production task.

The relationships between the system elements are not always correctly formulated and evaluated

The wrong regulating parameters are used to control organizational relationships

The main disadvantage of control over regulation is also evident in the company organization. Control can not react to faults. It can only be used effectively in very stable environments. If the system behavior permits feedback then regulation takes place. But this does not necessarily mean that suitable parameters are being used for feedback. Unfortunately the tendency is to use easily quantifiable but not necessarily decisive adjustment variables.

Do we use the correct adjustment variables for corporate control procedures?

The technique of regulation as such offers a well-developed set of tools. However, it

We must bear in mind that the behavior of control loops is not usually linear

requires a linearization of system behavior for the sake of simplification. But as we have already observed, real systems always reveal non-linear behavior patterns if they are not regarded and operated within very narrow confines. The idea of designing a factory consisting of autonomous control loops can not extend beyond this. It should not be surprising, then, if such a system proves to be unstable.

The key question is therefore how to proceed for best results when structuring an organization. From the analogy to natural systems one could draw the conclusion that the process should take place of its own accord. This consideration - 'how can a company *run itself?'* rather than 'how should a company *be run?'* is basically quite correct - but only in very narrow terms. The following can often be observed when new companies are established: a small - usually homogeneous - group of like-minded people work in a non-hierarchical atmosphere, united by a common vision. After a very short time the tasks are divided up in such a way as to deal with the work arising in an optimum manner. This takes place informally as part of an on-going process of learning, without organizational planning and job descriptions. This is precisely the advantage over established competitors that makes it possible for newcomers to assert themselves.

We must answer the question: how can a company run itself?

Initially, a new company benefits from learning through self-organization

As a company grows, traditional, rigid attitudes take over

As a rule, however, this situation can only be maintained for a short time. Examples such as the computer manufacturer Apple show that there is a tendency to move towards traditional methods of company management after a few years. This process seems to be inevitable, but we should note that competitiveness often suffers as a result.

One structural proposal that has been advanced recently is the concept of manufacturing segmentation. Above all, this involves the reorganization of existing production structures, namely the flow process. The major characteristics of segmentation are indicated by the keywords market and goal orientation, product orientation and cost consciousness. This approach demands the formation of new units and the transfer to them of additional functions, whilst several stages of the manufacturing process are grouped together from a point of view of organization.

With the segmentation approach previously dislocated functions are reintegrated into the value-creation chain

"Manufacturing segmentation also makes a new kind of operational structure possible and brings about a change in the concept of control. The goal is a form of group organization which carries the overall cost responsibility for a given product or segment. The change in the operational structure enables simple information and scheduling systems to be used and therefore facilitates the transfer of planning activities to the organizational unit."   [Wildemann 1988]

Marc S. Blaxill and Thomas M. Hout, Vice Presidents of the Boston Consulting Group, report on the turn-around of a niche manufacturer of high pressure hoses and pipes:

The typical weaknesses of many manufacturing structures - high overheads and long lead times - are often combatted with purely technical means

"The company tried first to solve the problem - high overhead costs, long lead times - by introducing a new MRP II system. But this only made things worse because the system masked the company's poor process control. For instance, one machining process had many unnecessary inventory holding points. Instead of simplifying the process and eliminating unwanted inventory, the MRP II system computerized the existing inventory needs.

The anticipated improvements did not materialize

Having made no progress, management took another tack. It examined all processes - customer service, order entry, fabrication and assembly, production planning and scheduling - and concluded that the aerospace and industrial product groups each had unique customer requirements. Aerospace products typically had low-volume production runs; industrial products fit a high-volume, make-to-stock business model.

Identify product groups and process them in separate business divisions

The company separated the two businesses and used flow charts to redesign each unit's processes. It used cellular manufacturing processes to improve coordination between processing steps, and it gave product teams the responsibility for shepherding products through design and manufacturing.

Manageable business units produce better results

This physical separation worked well. Two years into the change program, lead times for aerospace products fell from 20 weeks to 12 weeks, while industrial products lead times went from several weeks to just 3 days. On-time delivery was up from 15% to 80%; scrap and customer returns were down 42% and 60%, respectively; and sales were up 30%. Changing the process cut total overhead by 20%, which included the elimination of a 23-person quality-assurance team.

The same principles can be applied to all niche companies, no matter what their structure or how fast their growth. Indeed, it may be the most successful niche companies that need to worry most about manufacturing processes. If they are growing rapidly and are

not dealing with the threat of robust competitors, they are putting their futures at risk."
[Blaxill 1991]

It is debatable whether a reorganization which concentrates on specific target variables, such as lead time reduction, flow optimization or market orientation, can be sustainable in the long term - especially in view of the increasingly dynamic nature of manufacturing conditions. Changing the nature of the target can, on the other hand, reveal structures which have been statically reorganized and are therefore rigidly defined to be a dangerous impediment, especially if a great deal of effort was expended on optimization. Thus the crucial question remains: which notions should provide the basis for our organizational structures?

Structures are static, so how can we create a dynamic organization?

More knowledge - less plannability

Since the middle of the present century the total of available human knowledge has been increasing by leaps and bounds. The time required for our knowledge to double fell from its previous level of a hundred years to a mere six years (fig. 34). This explosive development is understandable once we realize that 90 percent of all scientists who have ever taught or undertaken research live in the present time. When we take a detailed look, we find that these scientists are responsible for amazing feats: they discover and publish a new chemical formula every minute, a new physical law every three minutes and a new medical insight every five minutes.

Knowledge is increasing progressively, since we have never had so much capacity for knowledge acquisition

In the year 1665 there was only one scientific journal published in the whole world The

Philosophical Translations of the Royal Society'. Two hundred years later, in 1865, there were already 1,000 journals. And in the hundred years from 1865 to 1965 this number rose to 100,000 with more than five million contributions. The precise number of scientific journals being published today is not known. But it is estimated that between 15 and 20 million scientific publications appear each year, although some of these are not really new.

New knowledge devalues the old

The "half life" of scientists and engineers is decreasing and must be compensated for through a constant process of learning

Of course, with each new publication some existing knowledge loses its value, becomes obsolete and unusable. Old insights and knowledge content, which have in many cases long been regarded as absolute and unshakeable become worthless in the train of rapid advances in science and lead all those who continue to work with them into a cul-de-sac. This effect can be expressed in terms of the 'half life' of scientists and engineers. According to experts in this field, they have lost half of their value five years after completion of their studies, unless

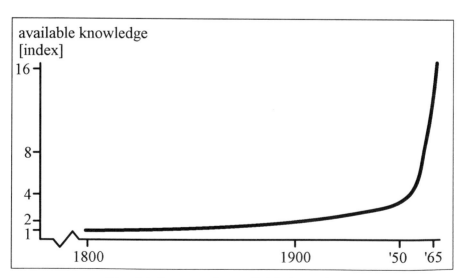

Fig. 34: Increase in available knowledge

their knowledge has been constantly updated in the interim. The need for a lifetime of learning therefore presents a challenge not only for each individual in his professional life, but also for the company and its organization. Each supplier must constantly ask himself if he has adequate know-how regarding his range of products and their manufacture when compared to the competition. And when resources are limited, as is usually the case, these must be concentrated accordingly.

If, as an initial approximation, we distinguish between the two directional thrusts of 'better' and 'cheaper', we can, for example, identify the manufacturers of scientific instruments or niche suppliers in the automotive industry, whose survival depends primarily on product know-how and less on manufacturing know-how. Other automobile manufacturers such as VW, Opel and Fiat, however, can not survive without supremacy in manufacturing know-how, e.g. in automation. In view of the rate at which knowledge is increasing, it is becoming more and more difficult, and expensive, to maintain know-how across the whole spectrum of the enterprise. This inevitably results in the need to concentrate on key or core areas. But then it is essential for the survival of the company to assess the future of a chosen area at the particular production site. Does it offer adequate potential for product and/or manufacturing innovation (fig. 35)?

Survival through product know-how or manufacturing expertise?

A single company can not encompass the whole range of necessary knowledge

Events are often non-linear and multicausal. In order to grasp them we simply restrict the scope of our observation and exclude external influences. This enables us to record, describe and even quantify events. However, linear extrapolations into the future often deviate very quickly

Our imagination can not cope with more than three variables at the same time

from real life. Man seems to be only able to relate linear variables unequivocally with each other, and is probably incapable of imagining more than three. Amongst consultants this is quite marked, since in portfolio analyses they often reduce the world to two variables, or if they really go into depth, to three.

It is generally accepted that knowledge and learning hardly have any effect if they are not put to practical use. More than anything else, a company offers the opportunity to integrate learning, planning and practical application. It is true that the learning process as such is slowed down by this, since all participants must be included in the process, but the loss is compen-

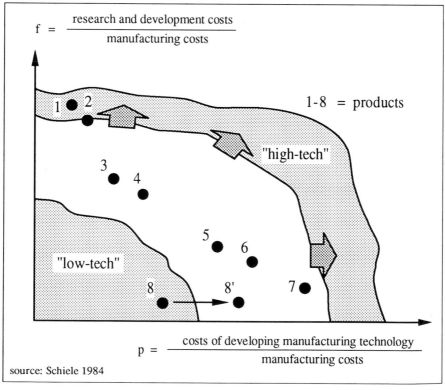

$$f = \frac{\text{research and development costs}}{\text{manufacturing costs}}$$

1-8 = products

"high-tech"

"low-tech"

$$p = \frac{\text{costs of developing manufacturing technology}}{\text{manufacturing costs}}$$

source: Schiele 1984

Fig. 35: Product qualification diagram

sated for by an increase in the probability of obtaining concrete learning results. Above all, the decision makers in a company must adjust their mental attitudes accordingly. They must understand that knowers, planners and doers must all be involved simultaneously through group work, workshops and the like. The focus here is always on specific company problems viewed as tasks to be solved. In a highly involved learning process - which affects both the active party and the person concerned - a new and individual corporate culture must be allowed to develop, in which internal frictions and waste - above all waste of human energy - are minimized.

Joint learning processes are gaining in importance in the search for company-specific solutions

Service in competition - we are all suppliers and customers

Manufacturing structures with a perspective for the future have to take account of a series of initial conditions. At this stage we shall take a brief look at some of the more important aspects. They are simply indispensible if we are to continue to play an important role in competitive international markets.

We must regard manufacturing as a service

An essential feature of manufacturing structures with a future is a consistently customer-oriented approach, or put in a nutshell:

Manufacturing is service.

Under 'service' we find in the dictionary:

"Services can in general be taken to signify all economic goods which serve to satisfy human needs after the manner of wares (tangible goods) ... They are often referred to as intangible goods. This general definition is

> controversial, since e.g. the provision of services can be made permanent, durable and almost of unlimited use by the aid of tangible goods and does not always do justice to the definitive features of the complex nature of services." [Brockhaus 1988]

There is no clear definition of 'service'

The uncertainty expressed in this definition persists in statistical works. In macroeconomic accounting the distinction between various sectors of the economy (primary, secondary and tertiary sectors) is made by reference to examples.

The use of the term 'service' to refer to the internal and external relationships of a manufacturing organization has become more and more frequent in recent years. A simple observation will shed some light on this: many companies are now entrusting company tasks to outsiders. For a long time now, this has applied to much more than just the company canteen - for example, those companies who have their tooling or data processing done out of house. And these are indeed classic service activities. It therefore follows that similar activities carried out within the company can and must also be classified as services. But more important than the establishment of terminology is the philosophy behind it. When it is applied to corporate procedures it can produce useful aids to optimization.

More important than the definition is the philosophy of service: an obligation must be fulfilled immediately, defects are not permitted, the customer does not have to wait and subsequent repairs are not possible

One thing has long been a part of daily routine in international companies but is still new to many small businesses: unrestricted national and international competition. The removal of trade barriers in the process of European unity will have consequences which many of those affected are still unaware of. Foreign competitors will very quickly and systematically work their way into the last domains and refuges of domestic markets. Soon barriers such as those of communications and logistics will be removed. Whoever wants to have the edge in this environment must have a genuine competitive advantage which he can call his own.

Manufacturers who see themselves as providers of a service for the benefit of the customer have a clear market advantage

Such a competitive edge is achieved by providing a better service for one's customers. An example from the former German Democratic Republic gives food for thought: after the market had been opened up some companies and products were virtually boycotted. This was not merely due to curiosity of the unknown nor was it simply a desire for better things that was responsible. It was simply the arrogance which a monopoly supplier had established over decades that was reason enough for customers to go to the competition. Even if this situation has now stabilized, the following principle is still valid:

Even for service providers the tendency is: operating resources wait for orders and not vice versa

"Offer your customers a service which is objectively better than your competitors'. This will ensure your long-term success."

Performance - this should be common knowledge by now - is not only judged by price. Not even objectively quantifiable variables such as defect rate and the ability to keep to deadlines are sufficient to describe it. A psychological aspect must be added: the way one treats one's customers, one's conduct as the purveyor of a service. Successful salesmen are aware of this, of course, but there is still a lot to learn.

The price is not everything. A great deal of psychology is involved

The subject of this book, however, is not the best way to market a product. Rather, it is concerned with the question of how to structure the

We must help to establish the principle of service

manufacturing process of a factory. The thesis is that here, too, we must allow the principle of service to come to the fore. It is not only a matter of reorganizing the functional divisions of a company into business processes; above all it is a question of corporate culture. This is where the greatest shortcomings and restrictions, but also the greatest opportunities, are to be found.

Only 20 % of employees use their full potential at work

From experience I would claim that in traditional organizational structures only 10 to 20 percent of employees work to their full potential. This is well known in management circles. They recognize this when a new problem arises and they find that there is only a small number of employees - usually the same ones - to whom they can entrust the task of finding a solution. They accept this as an inevitable consequence of the wide variety of human character and the broad spectrum of human behavior. Yet the ultimate goal must be the exploitation of the *full* potential of *all* employees, their creativity, their knowledge and their ability.

The obstacles are management practice and bureaucratic organization

Labor is not deliberately withheld

Despite all identifiable changes in management practices amongst senior staff, some executives seem to remain firmly convinced that the workers have conspired to reach *'an agreement to withhold their labor from their employer'*. This was how Taylor had formulated it in his day and striven to help. The result was 'scientific management' with precise job description, specification and control (cf. p. 46). By implementing the sophisticated processes developed to this end it may be possible to run an organization, but it will never attain its maximum potential.

This kind of management is often justified by the claim that employees are either unwilling or unable to work competently and with commitment. But surely this judgement only applies to a very small percentage. What is more, it would also be illusory to try to reach and to integrate all employees by the same methods. If a large discrepancy is observed between company objectives and personal goals then it would be logical for the two to part. But are such discrepancies ever uncovered in our companies? Without going into greater detail, one thing is certain: if we can reach and integrate only 50 percent of our employees through better management and organization, then we have doubled or even tripled the potential and the power of the company.

Not all employees can be reached, but the effective power of a company can be doubled or tripled

Let us reaffirm this once more: the goal system for innovative production structures must be based on two basic principles:

- *consistent customer orientation in internal and external company relationships*

- *arousal and exploitation of the full potential of the entire workforce.*

Our objective must be to ensure internal and external customer-orientation and to release the full potential of the workforce

About eighty years ago industrial companies began to establish research and development departments in order to systematically obtain knowledge for new products and - a matter very closely related to this in a process-oriented industry - for new processes. Not until about 25 years ago did the manufacturing industry realize that product and process innovations are of the same order of importance. This led to the construction of central departments for manufacturing technology or process development. These have become ever more important, but one problem remains: using their capacity correctly.

Product and process innovation are of equal importance

The various divisions of a company must support themselves as far as possible through the demand for their own services

Duplication is not wasteful, but necessary. It is a means of competition and understanding

The desire to avoid all duplication restricts freedom and creative competition

Even in the future, the "chemistry" between people will remain an important aspect of the relationship with suppliers

They too must be structured in a 'market oriented' way, both internally and externally. This means today that their annual budget is financed about 20 percent centrally and 80 percent by contractors. So here, too, this activity is regarded as a service which can and must be called upon. The current capacity in a central division must not be greater than is necessary to provide such special knowledge and abilities which would be underused in the value creating sector alone, because they are also of interest to others. There must always be a strong tendency in favor of decentralization so as to minimize central capacities. It is wrong to assume that maximum efficiency is attained by avoiding all redundancy, for this in turn restricts freedom and prevents a degree of internal competition. Minor overlaps, particularly in the intellectual domain, are absolutely essential if teamwork and cooperation are to be successful.

As far as the number of suppliers is concerned, the familiar 80-20 rule ('20 percent of the input variables produce 80 percent of the result and vice versa') still applies. The majority of them only account for a small percentage of the total volume of purchases. In order to facilitate the integration of the supplier as a partner in matters of know-how, this number has to be reduced drastically. In the automobile industry in particular this is specified as an objective which must result in system suppliers in turn having to integrate the suppliers of individual components. Subcontractors are then incorporated into a periodic monitoring program operated by the customer. As far as the future is concerned, the most important aspect of this process will continue to be the 'chemistry' between the partners. The attitude of the partners is more important than the quality of his fixed assets. But this basis is very hard to establish and must be constantly nurtured.

Complexity and specialization

The customer is king. That is correct. The consequences often drawn from this insight, on the other hand, are not always correct. In recent years the increase in the number of variants has been given prominence as a feature of changing market relationships. Superiority in handling the resultant complexity of the production process has been perceived as the key to competitiveness. New computer systems seem to offer the best methods of meeting this challenge. It therefore seemed to be logical to focus on technologically oriented solutions such as CIM (computer integrated manufacturing). As has been seen, however, this does not provide a sure and economical means of mastering such complexity. The fact that this complexity is not even always necessary is still being overlooked by those research and development departments which concentrate on high-tech solutions. Let us examine the destructive processes which are at work here:

It is not possible to master complexity entirely by technical means, so in the first instance it must be avoided

After intensive market research, the marketing department reports increased customer demand for special extras and asks for a corresponding variant to be included in the product range. The development department is given the task of working out a technical solution to the problem. When it is ready for the market, the extras are subjected to a cost analysis. A surcharge is then calculated on the basis of higher material costs and additional processing and assembly stages. In this manner an additional product is added to

Sales and costing drive us towards complexity through variety

The costs of variety are usually underestimated, since they are the sum of many individual activities

the range. Some time later the sales department reports that the products are hard to sell because of their high price. This results in cost reduction programs, of which suppliers are the favorite target. And in many cases a great deal of effort is expended in obtaining minimal savings in material and processing. Because the required success is not forthcoming, the competitor's products are examined once more and reveal high quality features at a low selling price. The company's own calculations show that such a price can not cover costs. The results are despair and a partly irrational search for patent solutions. The inadequacy of the costing system, however, prevents the real source of the problem from being discovered, which is to be found in the complexity of the manufacturing process; a large number of variants results in corrrespondingly high expenditure for

- design and planning including all consequential costs
- logistic work for parts and spare parts management
- data processing systems in production control
- technical work for additional manufacturing facilities
- after-sales service arising from quality problems.

Direct manufacturing costs amount to only a fraction of the extra expense; costing all activities makes this clear

What is suspected by many parties concerned - and occasionally is self-evident, although corresponding action is not taken - is that materials and processing costs only constitute a fraction of the additional expense. The costs of handling the extra variants amount to much more (fig. 36).

The only solution to this is to reduce complexity, in other words to dispense with added extras which attract surcharges. But this does not mean that the customer must make do with a puritanical range of rudimentary product versions; in the new series the more sophisticated variant becomes the basic model and the new basic price is increased only by the additional costs for material and manufacture, which are usually minimal. Under these circumstances, the customers come flooding back. The well-informed reader will recognize this scenario from automobile industry: the surcharge policy of many a European manufacturer has repeatedly proven to be an own goal.

Surcharges for variants can be an own goal

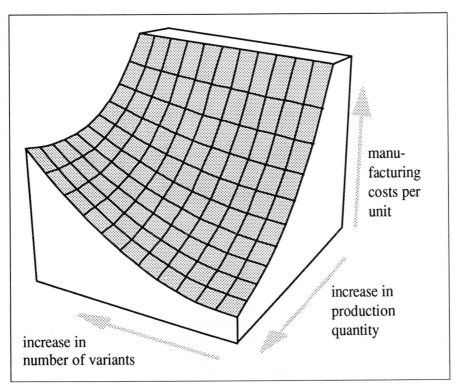

manu-
facturing
costs per
unit

increase in
production
quantity

increase in
number of variants

Fig. 36: The variant dilemma

Simplification and specialization are one way. The other is to control complexity when the market requires it

So the motto seems to be to reduce complexity. Zealous consultants are ready to offer their help in attaining this goal as quickly as possible. In many cases they are the same people who a few years ago were advocating the expansion of the product range as a hedge against the volatile nature of the market. The rapid succession of such changes in strategy is a consequence of unwarranted simplification. Complexity and its counterpart, specialization and simplicity, are two different types of product and production structure modifications which both hold great promise for the future.

The trend towards individuality must also be exploited

It can be shown that the prime objective of satisfying customer demands can be met even without a wide range of products. It should be obvious by now that such a product can under no circumstances be the smallest common denominator, in other words a minimal product specification. However, this solution is not

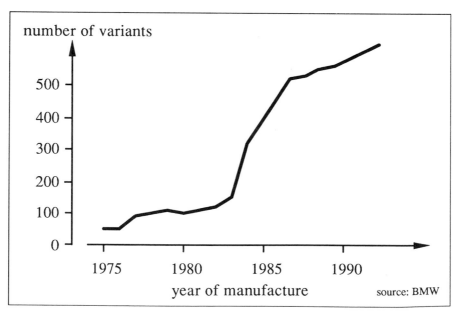

Fig. 37: Number of variants in automobile manufacture

applicable in the presence of highly sophisticated customer requirements. A status symbol
must be distinctive and demands individuality.
But in that case it can also be expensive.

The two alternatives of according priority to
scale (quantity) or scope (variety) in the product range must therefore be regarded as of
equal importance. Which to implement is not
merely a question of the current 'technical fad'
but must be decided upon on the basis of the
specific market situation. As we shall see,
selecting the one or other of these priorities is
an essential factor when designing the elements
of a factory with a future.

Scale and scope are the two crucial variables when designing an organizational structure

Of course we are now guilty of the kind of
simplification criticized above, reducing a complex situation to two essential variables. This is
permissible, however, for the sake of clarity
and furthermore we know that in *economies of
scale,* the quantity of goods produced has a
mathematically definable influence on manufacturing costs: the learning and experience curve
is fully exploited (cf. p. 48) and the one-off
costs of development, planning, special equipment, advertising, etc. are divided amongst a
large number of performance units. This gives
rise to the rule of thumb: double the quantity
equals 80 percent of the manufacturing costs
per unit.

Scale exploits the learning effect to the full. Double the quantity multiplies the unit production cost by 80 %

With regard to the relationship between cost
degression and increase in production quantity,
Blaxill and Hout distinguish between three
classes of business enterprise:

The *bureaucratic company* with a centralized
organizational structure in which specialized
departments carry out important support func-

tions. Its costing system is complex and structured in a formalized and hierarchical way.

The *niche company* which has a small number of product groups and because of its few levels of hierarchy can react fairly quickly to changing market demands.

Cost degression through scale varies according to company structure

The *robust company* which has successfully and reliably mastered its manufacturing processes and can react in a flexible way. Procedures have a process-oriented structure.

In all cases the law of quantity cost degression applies but when the production volume is doubled the unit production costs of the robust company fall by nearly 30 percent, in the case of the bureaucratic company and the niche company the reduction is only about 20 percent. The latter can therefore not profit from the effects of greater quantity (fig. 38).

A good market leader can not be beaten on cost and price

The concept of mass production is based on the quantity degression effect; this is why firms strive for high market shares and market dominance. Indeed, a market leader can not be beaten through accounting or pricing, provided he keeps abreast of developments and costs, unless one wishes to send prices into a nosedive and engage all competitors in a senseless price war resulting in high losses for one's own firm in the hope of being the only one to survive.

The problem area in economies of scope is to be found in information and communications. These difficulties must be overcome

In *economies of scope,* which result from the attempt to fulfil as many individual customer requirements as possible, in order to retain market shares the following happens:

- bottlenecks arise in information and communication
- the potential of the learning and experience curve can no longer be fully exploited

- additional work is always necessary and must be supported by a small number of products
- development and manufacturing processes must be handled more effectively
- 'time' is an essential factor in competition
- input and output stages are more critical than the actual process.

However, in economies of scale consistent quantity is often nothing more than a theoretical requirement which remains wishful thinking. It is rare for the quantity on which planning is based to be maintained over a prolonged period of time. The structural problem is that the two extremes of scale and scope require radically different attitudes and solutions for a given

Planning concepts are still dominated by a fictitious notion of the stability of scale manufacturing

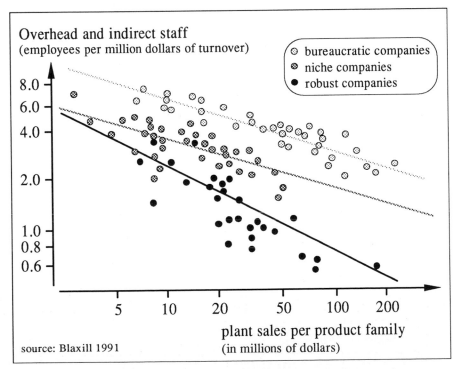

Fig. 38: Manufacturing overheads of different company types

company because the information and communication work involved in the two approaches is so different.

Scope must be resisted until as late as possible in the value-creation chain

In the first instance variants are to be avoided, in the second they must be mastered, technically and organizationally, by ensuring that they are created as late as possible in the manufacturing process, commercially by distinguishing processing costs from logistical costs.

However, it is essential to take into account the following points, which will lead us to a new concept:

Each subsystem of a factory should conform as far as possible to the principles of either scope or scale

- There is *one* best method for each manufacturing stage
- There is *no* best method for the manufacturing task.
- Only in the case of the distinct characteristics of *scale* or *scope* is there a best solution for processes, methods and facilities.
- A factory must therefore be structured in such a way that each subsystem places emphasis on either *scale* or *scope*.

variants

avoid variants

- query whether range is customer-oriented

- maximize the number of identical parts

- systematically reduce vertical range of manufacture

control variants

- create variants in final production stage

- create variants after despatch

Fig. 39: Tackling the variant dilemma

A further very important insight to be derived from this is that it is wrong to want to impose *one* method or *one* system in management, organization or technical solutions on a factory or even a corporation. In any given case this will bring about constraints without producing an ideal solution. It is only necessary to ensure that communication takes place at the relevant interfaces in real time, that is on a day-to-day basis, horizontally and vertically using coordinated data structures and information content. As a simple example of this, today no-one uses the same production control methods to organize his production or his tool and jig construction.

It is a mistake to organize a company, or even a concern, according to only one management method, one structural principle or one procedural system

Economy through	
quantity (Economy of Scale)	*variety* (Economy of Scope)
specialist quantity concentration know-how specialized work stations rigid automation	generalist organizational concentration information total processing flexible automation
manufacturing process (logistics) stable production quality through inspection	(manufacturing process) logistics product phase-in / phase-out quality through process control
hierarchical structures bureaucratic one large control loop consecutive	network structures group many small loops concurrent

Fig. 40: Economy of scale and economy of scope

The differing requirements are familiar to everybody. In manufacturing, however, there is a tendency to look for *one* single method for production control, although there, too, differing requirements and possible solutions apply to the various stages of manufacturing (fig. 41).

A variety of solutions, e.g. for production control, must be used within a company

The chosen method must be subjected to periodic quality inspection

If production units are designed to be as 'pure' as possible in accordance with the one or other of the two principles, this means:

- scale: concentration on market, product or process know-how; the amount of internal logistical work is insignificant.

- scope: concentration on communication between units; the amount of process work is insignificant.

Tailoring a company towards scale or scope also has a dynamic historical aspect. Using the example already introduced in Chapter 2 it is

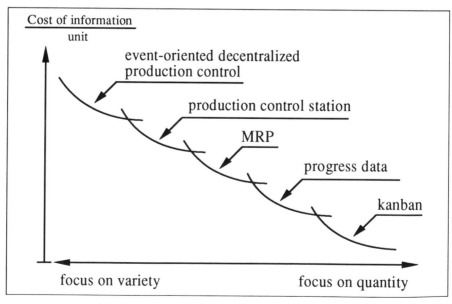

Fig. 41: Suitable methods of process control

possible to trace the shift of emphasis throughout the whole industrial age (cf. p. 50). Furthermore, this example illustrates once again the
growing pace of corporate organizational
development.

In a situation which is becoming increasingly
complex, any operation-oriented form of organization involving the division of labor must
inevitably lead to a persistent rise in overheads.
Cost reduction programs which concentrate on
this (e.g. through overhead cost value analysis)
only tackle the symptoms and do not deal with
the problem at the roots. In most cases the
reduction in overheads calculated on the basis
of indirect personnel is not achieved, since
'quarter and half heads' were added together as
potential economies and of course these can not
be dispensed with.

*Overhead cost
analysis is only
concerned with
symptoms; its suc-
cess is not very
far-reaching*

It is better to have an approach which illumi-
nates the manufacturing processes and their
effects on overheads in detail. Indirect personnel are only required when it is a question of
tasks which can not be performed directly
within the value-creation chain.

*We must redesign
the value-creation
process*

In their worldwide study of over 100 manufacturing companies, Blaxill and Hout demonstrate
that competitiveness is determined not by the
level of overheads, but by manufacturing processes [Blaxill 1991]. Expenses are incurred by
inefficient conditions, activities and processes
before, during and after the actual value creation phase. If we are in full control of the production processes, then all unnecessary or additional information processing is avoided, which
reduces personnel activity and overheads. In the
opinion of the authors not only are the overheads in 'robust manufacturing processes'

*Mastering the
production process
avoids unnecessary
information
processing and
ensures competi-
tiveness*

lower, but also lead times are shorter and quality is higher. Of course, it is necessary here to take into account all processes from the development stage to relationships with one's suppliers and customers, otherwise incorrect decisions may be the result:

Reducing the vertical range of manufacture without due thought can be disastrous

> As a negative example they quote a company in the USA which purchases some of the models in its product range from outside suppliers, in order to economize on overheads. However, since the goods purchased must be incorporated into the company's own operating procedures, they have the opposite effect of increasing overheads. These rise still further because of the extra logistics work involved in purchasing. In addition, all this results in surplus capacities whilst the company neglects to make any innovations of its own in manufacturing technology. So the company's competitiveness suffers, since it ends up with a worse state of technology and increased logistical expense.

> As a positive example, Toyota is cited, a company which employs fewer than one employee per million dollars of turnover, in other words, only a fifth of the workforce of comparable American competitors.

Examples illustrate the great potential for the integration of indirect activities into the value-creation process

> The corporation, 'Hashimoto Forming Industries' has such a good control of its rolling processes for laminated preforms that the number of indirect employees and salary-paid staff is less than 50 percent of those of a comparable American competitor. This is certainly due not only to the actual manufacturing process, but also to the integration of manufacturing into the overall process.

A major rethink and a whole new approach are therefore required. Otherwise costs *and* performance will be reduced piecemeal with a consequent loss of competitiveness. Function-oriented bureaucratically run companies will find themselves on the losing side in spite of all these cost-reduction programs if they are not prepared to undergo a process of rethinking, learning and restructuring which may indeed be lengthy but which nonetheless promises results.

Function-oriented, bureaucratically run companies are on the losing side

Information as a production factor

As early as the seventies, Gordon Moore, co-founder of the Intel corporation, had foreseen the rapid increase in performance and the drastic fall in price in the electronic components sector. This development was made possible by constant progress in the field of miniaturization.

Electronic components: rapid increase in performance accompanied by a sharp reduction in price

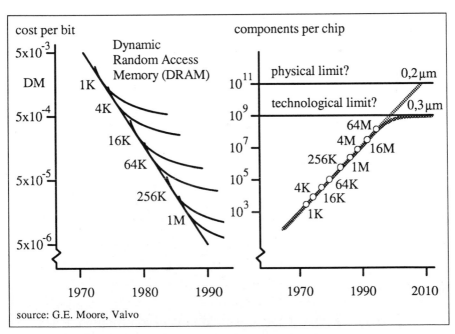

Fig. 42: Performance and cost of electronic components

The microstructures of today's chips are already below 10^{-6} m (fig. 42). We have already referred to the impact that this has had on manufacturing technology. Today, not even the most conservative company can avoid being affected by this trend, both in respect of the product and its manufacture.

Factories are information processing systems

Although this is not covered in terms of operational data acquisition, we must appreciate that

- a factory is an information processing system
- the amount of information processing has a decisive effect on manufacturing structure.

Main areas of application: technical and logistical information flow

We can distinguish between two essential areas of activity:

- technical information flow (product and process oriented)

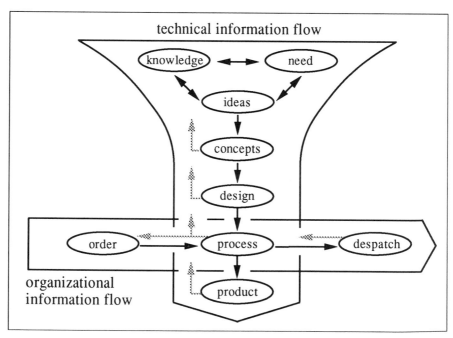

Fig. 43: Technical and logistical flow of information in a manufacturing company

- logistical information flow (procedure oriented).

The technical information flow from design and development through the planning stage to the process itself is still marked by the repeated acquisition of identical data, resulting in unnecessary duplication. All the information required for a geometric description of the product is contained in the CAD system, and this is precisely the information needed for example, to generate the paths of tools operated by industrial robots. And similarly, the technological data required for surface treatment and welding processes are also stored.

CAD is the point of departure for the rationalization of technical information flow

A common data model together with suitable data structures facilitates the integration of partial solutions. But it must also be possible for information flow in the opposite direction, so that knowledge or data acquired later can be fed back to the design and development stages to be amended and updated directly, even if

Integration of partial solutions through a universal data model

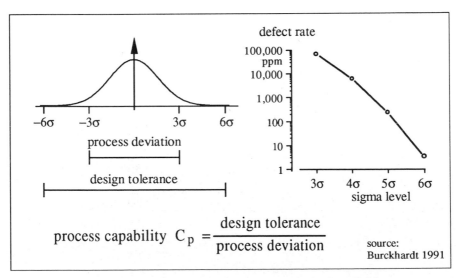

Fig. 44: Process capability as a statistical variable

only in a target performance comparison for quality assurance purposes. This short and rapid control loop must be complete, since the customer and the legislator are becoming less and less tolerant of defects.

Total quality with low information and processing requirements is economical

If we succeed in keeping manufacturing tolerances reliably within the permitted limits then the amount of information processing needed to assure quality is also kept to a minimum. With a process tolerance of six times the standard deviation, the quantity of defective parts is reduced to 3.4×10^{-6}. The desired goal is a process capability of $C_p \geqq 2$ (fig. 44). Whereas process deviation is the responsibility of manufacturing, design tolerance comes under the auspices of the product development division. This means that 'total quality' can be achieved economically, since information processing and production process work are reduced simultaneously. A new product must be better than the product it replaces at the very moment it

Striving for zero faults leads to the 6-sigma program, 3 faults per million, and to a robust, controlled process

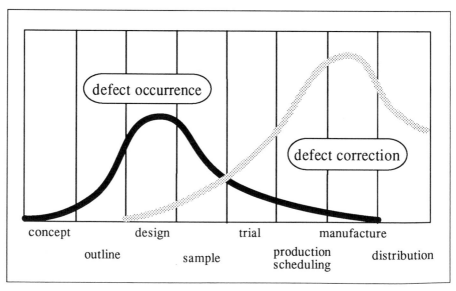

Fig. 45: Defect occurrence and correction

comes on the market. It is therefore essential to achieve stable production without quality defects as quickly as possible after production commences. In this way the costly delay between the occurrence and the detection of defects can be reduced to a minimum (fig. 45).

It is better to avoid defects than to rectify them

The logistical or organizational information flow comprises the path from the order being placed by the customer or determined by the sales program through the manufacturing process to the delivery of the goods, including invoicing. It is rationalized by the production planning and control system. Structures relying

The PPC system is the starting point for rationalization of the organizational information flow

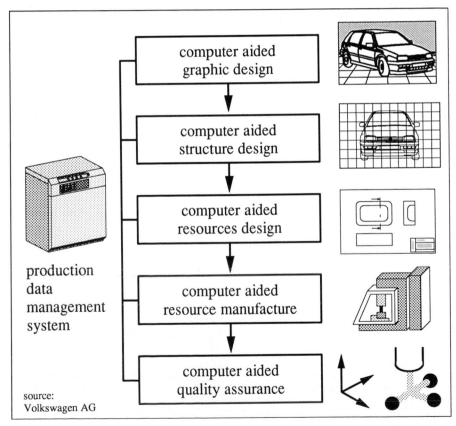

Fig. 46: Computer aided process chain in bodywork manufacture

The specialized organization of mass production requires little information processing

on extreme division of labor such as Taylor regarded as the apparently ideal solution are characterized by the low degree of information processing needed for process control. This information is available, it is true, but it is generally ignored, since it was determined once only, during job scheduling: the plate cam as a mechanically encoded information path or the arrangement of a production line as an expression of the sequence of work stages.

Customer-oriented manufacturing involves a large measure of logistics and communications work

Seen from the point of view of information technology, the amount of logistical and communication work is greater in a production system which focuses on variety, since, for example, neither the design of the workpiece nor the processing sequence are stored in the machine tool or the production equipment. The

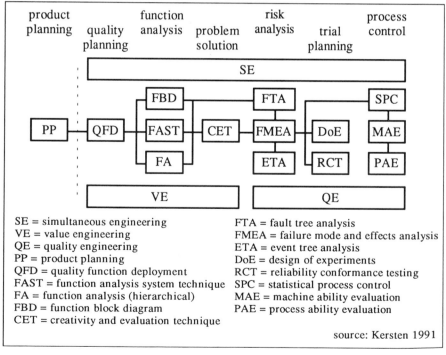

SE = simultaneous engineering
VE = value engineering
QE = quality engineering
PP = product planning
QFD = quality function deployment
FAST = function analysis system technique
FA = function analysis (hierarchical)
FBD = function block diagram
CET = creativity and evaluation technique

FTA = fault tree analysis
FMEA = failure mode and effects analysis
ETA = event tree analysis
DoE = design of experiments
RCT = reliability conformance testing
SPC = statistical process control
MAE = machine ability evaluation
PAE = process ability evaluation

source: Kersten 1991

Fig. 47: Integrated methods system

information is contained in a drawing or is electronically encoded and must be converted afresh each time. In order to structure the manufacturing process we nowadays have at our disposal a kit system consisting of various methods which should be combined and applied in a logical way. Just like each machine, each method has its own limited area of application. This means that a method should be selected specifically for a particular task and may have to be substituted in the event of changes in the basic conditions (fig. 47).

Defects can be prevented through simultaneous engineering. The methods are available

Manufacturing is the conversion of information into structured matter by means of controlled energy. Increased costs for data processing are resulting in a steady increase in cost-conscious-ness on the part of users in this field. The value of the production factor of information is receiving more and more recognition as a fourth resource. There is no doubt about the expedi-ency and necessity of electronic data processing for this purpose. But solutions are becoming more and more extensive and complex. Technical progress demands constant adapta-tion and consequently considerable effort is required on the part of data processing special-ists to maintain their competence.

Manufacturing is the conversion of information

Information is increasing in importance as a production factor

Controlling methods using full absorption cost-ing are therefore also being applied to the data processing sector. The knowledge that data processing tasks do not belong to the core activity of the company is leading to increased discussion about the question of obtaining these services externally. At the least, the service character of this division must be established internally by means of defined inputs and out-puts. For one thing is certain: a company must be in full control of, and successfully imple-

Data processing is either a service or a support function

ment, its own internal information and communication systems, since they are a decisive factor in competition. However, this does not exclude the possibility of purchasing the required hardware capacity externally through a network according to need and thereby taking advantage of the know-how of qualified full-time software engineers.

Information is a resource. We must not waste it

If information is to be seen as a factor in production then we must treat it just as rationally as we do the production factors of labor, capital and material. The view that we can be generous with information processing and storage because of the constantly increasing cost-effectiveness of hardware takes us down the wrong road. The opposite should be the case: the amount of information processing required to perform a manufacturing task should be kept to a minimum.

We must reduce the information processing required for a production task to a minimum

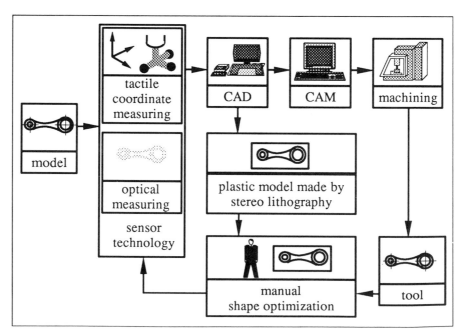

Fig. 48: CAQ information network

Unfortunately, attempts to capture 'information' as a cost factor after the fashion of material or wages do not seem to be successful. We can indeed record the quantity, for instance in terms of storage used, but as a rule we are not able to assign a value to the data or the information. So we are currently left only with a qualitative estimation and the need to structure procedures and systems in such a way as to require a minimum of information processing.

The cost of information can not be quantified

In future, we must be similarly critical of expert systems, or rather knowledge processing systems, although these can assist us in our venture to improve the structure of complex systems, since they provide a more rapid analysis of results.

The factory of the future?

The reader might now ask himself if he once again has a description of the 'factory of the future' in his hands. If this impression has been given, it is not too late to correct it.

A factory is always rooted in a social and technical environment. For this reason the location of a factory can necessitate quite different solutions in the light of otherwise identical requirements.

There can be no factory of the future in absolute terms

A factory must always be designed to operate as a function of its environment, sales market, purchasing market, labor market, infrastructure, etc. The question of the factory of the future can therefore only be answered with the recognition that this does not and will not exist as a definite concept. We are left with a variety of solutions whose characteristics are that they are suited to their environment and employ a

The design of a factory must reflect its environment

A factory with a future must be dynamic

dynamic force, i.e. constant internal and external innovations, to ensure that we have, in an environment becoming ever more turbulent, 'factories *with* a future'.

As we have seen from our trip through the world of industrial production so far, the number of approaches which seem promising in the long run is very small, whereas we are faced with a constant proliferation of tasks and problems. How right this assertion is can be seen most clearly in the field of organizational design, which is vitally important from a strategical point of view. It appears that this area represents the limits of the engineer's scientific cognitive capacity.

In order to design such structures we need new insights and approaches. Does nature provide us with models?

Highly complex structures in a turbulent environment require a suitable scientific description and explanation. But engineering is not alone in being confronted by this truth. For quite some time now, certain areas of science have been working on new paradigms to deal with the conditions and behavior patterns of just such 'chaotic systems'. These activities are directed towards producing models and theories which can be described and explained.

The Fractal Factory: Stability and order must always be recreated out of turbulence and randomness

The following sections of this chapter are intended to provide an insight into these works, whereby we do not wish to lose sight of our own main point of interest, namely the matter of establishing organizational structures. We should take proposals offered by other branches of science very seriously, and should carefully examine how far they can be applied to our own problems. Even the cybernetic system theory, the basis of many economic and technological theories, came originally from quite a different area of research - biology. We have taken to heart the requirement to cast our gaze beyond the limits of our discipline to the extent that it has already found its way into the nomenclature of our experiment. We refer to the **Fractal Factory.**

"Fractals are a descriptive system and a new methodology for an investigation that has only just begun. They may also be, like the hologram, a new image of wholeness. Over the next decade fractals will undoubtedly reveal more and more about the chaos hidden within regularity and about the ways in which stability and order can be born out of underlying turbulence and chance. And they will reveal more about the movements of wholeness."   [Briggs 1989]

But new concepts need time to prove themselves

Order and chaos - two complementary views of the world

In the year 1892 the French mathematician Henri Poincaré (1854-1912) made a strange discovery. During his attempt to predict planetary orbits whilst taking account of their influences on each other, he arrived at some interesting conclusions: a minimal deviation in the initial variables of the calculation resulted in widely deviating results. This discovery distressed the scholar because it destroyed the view of the world that was held at that time.

According to the psychologist, Edward de Bono, you can not dig a new hole if you continue to dig the same one deeper. You must go and dig elsewhere

"Things are so bizarre that I can no longer bear to think about them."   [Henri Poincaré]

Ever since antiquity a deterministic view of the world based on the principle of causality and dual logic has dominated the thoughts and

Our intellectual tradition: analyze, insist on a point of view and look for errors

actions of Western science. This was based on the insights of logical-rational thinking and a rejection of the mysticism of the Pre-Socratic area, inseparably linked with the names of two Greek philosophers, Socrates' pupil, Plato (427-347 B.C.) and above all Plato's pupil, Aristotle (384-322 B.C.). The philosophical principles of rationalism, partly submerged under the outpourings of Christian mystics in the Middle Ages, experienced their renaissance in the age of Humanism and culminated in the radical theories of knowledge of the Enlightenment philosopher, René Descartes (1596-1650) ('cogito, ergo sum' - 'I think, therefore I am'). Pierre Simon Laplace (1749-1827) proclaimed the fundamental predictability of the future, provided that the state of the universe and all its laws were known at a specific point in time.

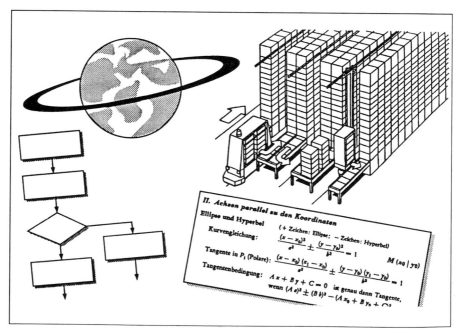

Fig. 49: Deterministic view of the world

This approach has bestowed a great many successes on the natural sciences and technology, too, has had its share of the benefits. We seemed to be on the verge of an explanation of the final secrets of nature; optimism amongst scholars knew no bounds. There were even those who predicted the end of entire branches of science because all relationships would be explained before too long (when he was in the ninth grade, Max Planck was advised not to study physics for this reason! [Sexl 1984]).

Faith in predictability has brought great successes

Real events very quickly deviate from our linear extrapolations

Frederic Winslow Taylor, the founder of production engineering as a scientific discipline clearly belonged to this school of thought:

"By means of four quite elaborate slide rules, which have been especially made for the purpose of determining the all-round capacity of metal-cutting machines, a careful analysis was made of every element of this machine in

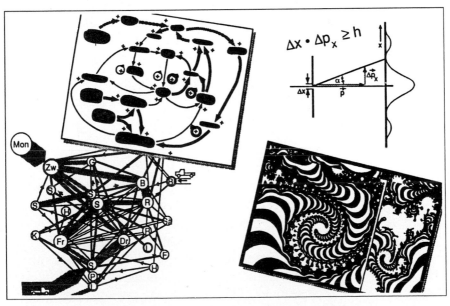

Fig. 50: Chaotic view of the world

Linearity can only be presumed within very narrow limits

We can continue to predict things in limited systems

We must dispense with causality and the sovereignty of logic as the only principle

its relation to the work in hand. Its pulling power at its various speeds, its feeding capacity, and its proper speeds were determined by means of the slide rules, and changes were then made in the countershaft and driving pulleys so as to run at its proper speed. Tools, made of high-speed steel, and of the proper shapes, were properly dressed, treated and ground."   [Taylor 1911]

Whilst engineering science today still seems to cling to this fiction, natural scientists were obliged to abandon it decades ago in the light of some surprising observations. The theory of relativity and quantum mechanics bade farewell to the principle of causality. If it is fundamentally impossible to describe states unequivocally and if it follows from this uncertainty that it is impossible to predict the behavior of a system, then a new view of the world is required. It is well known that the scholars of the time were plunged into a deep spiritual crisis because the new view of the world also had strong repercussions on matters of philosophy.

The following gives an insight into the thoughts of two historical luminaries on chance and determinism.

Laplace, 1776
"The present state of the system of nature is evidently a consequence of what it was in the preceding moment, and if we conceive of an intelligence which at a given instant comprehends all the relations of the entities of this universe, it could state the respective positions, motions and general affects of all these entities at any time in the past or future... The simplicity of the law by which the celestial

bodies move, and the relations of their masses and distances, permit analysis to follow their motions up to a certrain point; and in order to determine the state of the system of these great bodies in past or future centuries, it suffices for the mathematician that their position and their velocity be given by observation for any moment in time. Man owes that advantage to the power of the instrument he employs, and to the small number of relations that it embraces in its calculations.

Order and determinism: the predictable relationship between cause and effect

Poincaré, 1903
"A very small cause which escapes our notice determines a considerable effect that we can not fail to see, and then we say that the effect is due to chance. If we knew exactly the laws of nature and situation of the universe at the initial moment, we could predict exactly the situation of that same universe at a succeeding moment. But even if it were the case that the natural laws had no longer any secret for us, we could still only know the initial situation approximately. If that enabled us to predict the succeeding situation with the same approximation, that is all we require, and we should say that the phenomenon had been predicted, that it is governed by laws. But it is not always so; it may happen that small differences in the initial conditions produce very great ones in the final phenomena. A small error in the former will produce an enormous error in the latter. Prediction becomes impossible, and we have the fortuitous phenomenom."   [Crutchfield 1986]

Chaos and probability: unpredictable relationship between cause and effect

Predictions can become impossible; the result is 'random'

The butterfly effect: a minor disturbance can cause a tornado in another place

Poincaré's discovery was forgotten for almost a hundred years. Laborious manual calculations were a severe limitation to anyone wishing to pursue these phenomena further. It was not until the advent of the computer that a new approach for dealing with complex systems could be developed. This was prompted by, amongst other things, a chance discovery. In mathematical models used to describe weather conditions it was shown that minor deviations in apparently insignificant parameters could reverse the results. This behavior has become known as the so-called butterfly effect; model calculations show that the beat of a butterfly's

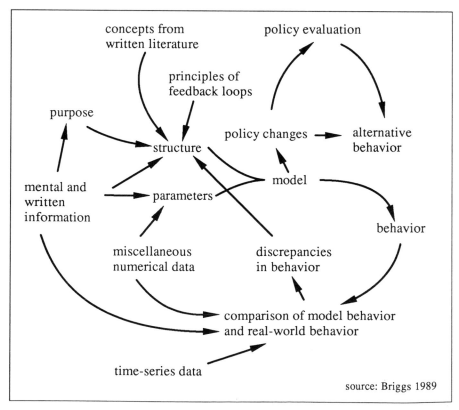

Fig. 51: Non-linear feedback in model formation

wings can trigger off a tornado on another continent. Although this effect can never actually be demonstrated in reality, it does convey an idea of what chaos actually is and where the differences to the use of the term in everyday language lie.

In corporate practice such effects have for some time been received with an air of helplessness. In this connection, people speak of an extrapolation trap without having any conclusive answers to the questions this throws up (fig. 52).

The behavior of complex systems leads us again and again into an extrapolation trap

The weather patterns in our atmosphere are ideally suited as a model for studying the behavior of complex systems. Although each air particle alone is subject to strict physical laws, structures of a higher order, e.g. high and low pressure areas are formed. Now, we may ask how such structures, created out of nothing as it were, can come about in extremely complex systems. Answers to this question bring us closer to the solution which concerns us here, the creation of forward-looking manufacturing systems. The symptoms are indeed comparable.

We must change our way of thinking, overcome our prejudices. Such stereotypes are purely reactive, negative and today they can even be destructive

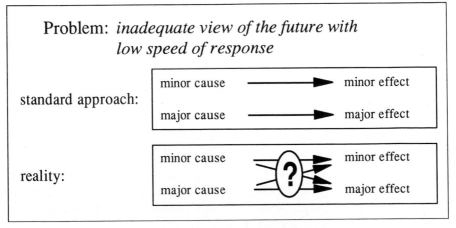

Fig. 52: The extrapolation trap

Complex systems will become transparent if we can find and harness the crucial regulating parameters

A complex system is described by reference to its elements, their characteristics and their interactions with each other. Also, they interact with their environment, since real systems can not be treated as self-contained units. Of course, a complete description of the system must include details on an atomic scale and the behavior of the system in time relative to environmental influences (control parameters) is expressed by a correspondingly vast number of non-linear differential equations. This fact is somewhat shocking and even discouraging to those who would seek to describe the system, or even to influence it. However, the fact that structures of a higher order are nevertheless formed in such systems can also be expressed as a mathematical derivative:

Regulating parameters always restore order from chaos. They enable self-organization

Some state parameters are subject to rapid change, whilst others change only slowly. When describing macrostructures, those parameters which change very rapidly can be ignored. This reduces the number of equations to be solved. Now, it can be shown that even in complex systems this long-term behavior is often dependent on only a small number of parameters. We shall refer to these parameters as regulating parameters. Their equations are the key to the description of macroscopic orders and the stationary solutions of these equations describe a macrostructure which may be present. In determining and influencing the regulating parameters, not the control parameters, lies the key to understanding and controlling complex systems. This is not only true of natural structures but also applies to phenomena in organizational development. What interests us particularly in this connection is a phenomenon generally referred to as self-organization.

Structure formation through self-organization

The formation of well-ordered system structures can be described by reference to numerous examples. The obvious parallel in this connection is, of course, that of living organisms. Here we are dealing with extremely complex, interlinked order structures which defy static description. At least, systems of this kind can not be interpreted on the basis of a simple pattern of cause and effect. Life organizes itself. Friedrich Cramer refers to the self-organization of matter into life as a physical principle.

Order in life: dynamic creation and decay with constant self-organization

> "In order to maintain this order in the dynamical system, structuring processes must be constantly operative in order to compensate for the constant decomposition which inevitably accompanies life."

> "Structure formation by 'self-organization' can be found, for example, if we dissect water polyps into two parts, or if we cut a piece out of the middle of one. Within 48 hours a section of the tissue, which at first seemed fairly uniform, grows into a new head. The first process in the creation of a head is the formation of a 'morphogenetic field': in a few hours the future head area is 'activated' ... and this activation, which is at first invisible, subsequently results in the formation of a new head." [Cramer 1989]

Further analogies to structure formation can be seen amongst synergetic processes.

The laser has opened a remarkable new range of applications since its development 30 years ago and has in the meantime become an indispensible manufacturing tool. But we shall

Synergetics in the laser: the interplay between random-ness, the formation of many waves and necessity. The pre-ferred wave assimilates its weaker competi-tors

not be concerned here so much with its applications as with its physical basis.

A laser differs from traditional gas discharge tubes in that it has two mirrors which ensure that the light waves stay in the tube for as long as possible before they are beamed out through one of the partially translucent mirrors. The light waves force stimulated luminous electrons to oscillate and to amplify the wave until it has passed on all its energy to the wave. Waves of different frequencies compete with each other to assimilate the energy of the electrons. The latter, however, 'prefer' waves which best approximate their own 'inner dance beat'. The preferred wave is now amplified in a kind of snowball effect and finally gains the upper hand and once it has assumed the role of 'regulator' it forces all newly stimulated electrons to oscillate in time with the same beat.

"To make all the electrons oscillate at the same frequency, a regulator, namely a light wave, must be present. However, the light wave itself is only the product of regular electron oscillations. It looks as though we must first engage the services of a higher power to first create the initial state of order, so that this can then maintain itself. But this is, as we have just seen, not the case. First of all a kind of competition took place, a process of selection in which all electrons became the slave of a particular wave. What is interesting here is that the various waves were at first created spontaneously and at random by the electrons and that they were subsequently filtered out and selected according to the basic laws of competition. What we have before us is the interplay

> between chance and necessity which is typical of synergetics, whereby 'chance' is represented by spontaneous emission and 'necessity' is embodied in the unrelenting law of competition."   [Haken 1986]

Fig. 53 represents the various stages in the formation of light waves in an incandescent electric light on the one hand and a laser on the other. Matchstick men standing next to a canal create waves on the surface of the water by dipping sticks into it. If they do this independently of each other, the result is merely an erratically moving surface, corresponding to the light waves generated by an electric light bulb. However, if the stimulation is regular, an equally regular wave is produced, analogous to the coherent emissions of laser light.

Laser light: an example of a self-organizing system

The similarity between these processes and events in a factory is unmistakable. The traditional view sees manufacturing as taking place according to the principle of coherence, but - and this is the crucial distinction - in response to central commands. Whilst this principle worked quite well on an ancient galley, because

Synergetics applied to manufacturing; the factory must evolve from a galley to the league of speedboats

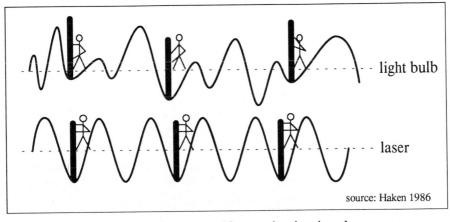

light bulb

laser

source: Haken 1986

Fig. 53: Analogy to self-organization in a laser

it had to, or would do so for a short period on a rowing boat, a factory actually corresponds more to the former model: uncoordinated individual activities.

Vision of the factory with a future: based on the principle of self-organization

Must not a vision of the factory with a future conform rather to the latter principle based on self-organization? All elements act together, steered only by regulating parameters, and thereby produce a cost-effective output.

The world of fractals

The fractal: a measure for highly complex structures

Ever since scientists began to study the laws of dynamic changes, the phenomenon of self-organization, they have tried to create qualitative instruments for this turbulent field. The breakthrough was made in mathematics, which discovered a measure for highly complex structures: the fractal.

The problem of describing and analyzing geometric objects in multidimensional spaces has occupied mathematicians for 200 years. Differential geometry describes small regions of these structures, which when seen in their totality are often very complex, by means of simple forms such as lines or planes [cf. Müssigmann 1992].

Scaling behavior: how do the details of the structure appear under magnification?

Many natural structures have long seemed to defy mathematical descriptions because of their irregular and jagged shapes. Neither Euclidean geometry nor calculus provide suitable tools for dealing with them. This becomes clear when we investigate scaling behavior: 'smooth' objects become simpler the more we enlarge them, whereas natural objects reveal more and more detail. We refer to this phenomenon as non-trivial scaling behavior (fig. 54).

Such structures are the subject of the Theory of Fractal Geometry [Mandelbrot 1987] devised by Benoit B. Mandelbrot (b. 1925). Mandelbrot calls the objects of this geometry 'fractal'. The term is derived from the latin, 'fractus' (broken, fragmented). With this Mandelbrot opens up possibilities for the mathematical treatment of natural fractal shapes whose coarseness and structure remain basically the same when resolution is increased. The main characteristic of these structures is therefore that each of their parts incorporates the whole of the structure.

Fractal structures: the whole structure is reflected in each detail

We can find numerous and varied examples of fractal shapes: broken edges of metals, mountain formations, coastlines. Even phenomena such as the rise and fall of prices on the stock exchange appear in a totally new light when viewed as fractals. The impetus for Mandelbrot's work originated from the observation of such forms. In a nutshell, the advantage of this method of observation can be described as follows:

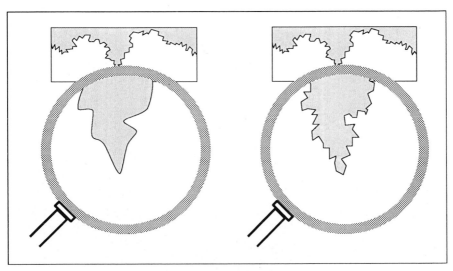

Fig. 54: Trivial and non-trivial scaling behavior

Fractal geometry enables a mathematical description of complex natural forms

"Fractal geometry is a new language. Once you can speak it, you can describe the shape of a cloud as precisely as an architect can describe a house."   [Barnsley 1988]

The American physicist F.J. Dyson summarizes the development of fractal geometry in the following way:

In mathematics, too, a revolution has taken place in the 20th century

"*Fractal* is a word invented by Mandelbrot to bring together under one heading a large class of objects that have played an historical role in the development of pure mathematics... Classical mathematics had its roots in the regular geometric structures of Euclid and the continuously evolving dynamics of Newton. Modern mathematics began with Cantor's set theory and Peano's space-filling curve. Historically, the revolution was forced by the discovery of mathematical structures that did not fit the patterns of Euclid and Newton... The mathematicians regarded them as important in showing that the world of pure mathematics contains a richness of possibilities going far beyond the simple structures that they saw in Nature. Twentieth-century mathematics flowered in the belief that it had transcended completely the limitations imposed by its natural origins.

Theoretically developed mathematical structures can be found in natural objects

Now - as Mandelbrot points out, Nature has played a joke on the mathematicians. The 19th-century mathematicians may have been lacking in imagination, but Nature was not. The same structures that the mathematicians invented to break loose from 19th-century naturalism turn out to be inherent in familiar objects all around us."   [Dyson 1978]

The aesthetic attraction derived from fractal objects is strengthened even further by their simple mathematical description [cf. Peitgen 1986]. Through repeated application of very simple rules of calculation self-similar structures arise with a high degree of organization.

The most familiar fractal object is the Mandelbrot set (fig. 55). It is derived from number sequences in the complex number range as a result of the formula $z(n+1) = [z(n)]^2 + c$. The shape of this set marks the area in which the number sequences remain bounded. Enlarged sections always reveal similar, but never identical, structures.

Relatively simple mathematical rules produce complex self-similar structures when iteration is applied

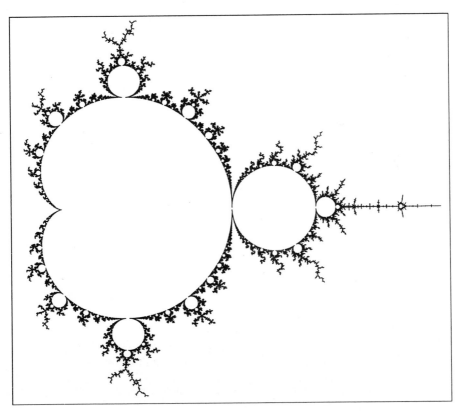

Fig. 55: The Mandelbrot set

It was computers that first revealed the expressive power of fractal geometry

In order to generate such images a large number of iterations are usually necessary. Not only does the computer seem to be predestined for this task, it has become an indispensible tool. Without computers, the expressive power of this new description of phenomena would never have been recognized nor proven.

Today, fractal geometry is used as a tool in many branches of science

Because of the extremely close relationship between fractals on the one hand and the structure of many natural phenomena on the other it is not surprising that fractal geometry has already found its way into other areas of science. Amongst them are physics, chemistry, biology, statistics, astronomy, meteorology and even economics [cf. Müssigmann 1992].

Characteristics of fractal objects: self-organization, self-similarity and dynamics

We can discern two prime characteristics of fractal objects: self-organization and self-similarity. Furthermore we have seen that the feedback mechanisms in fractal formation generate an amazing diversity of shapes, which are an expression of the highly *dynamic* nature of the process.

After the stock-taking we have done in the first and second chapters it is now time to derive a basic pattern from these structures which we can use in the design of industrial corporations.

4. The Fractal Factory - an Integrating Approach

Really new ideas open the way for new potential solutions, but they also create new problems. We are not afraid of this; if you do not move, you can not move anything else. And we have shown in detail that we *must* all move. We therefore have to reach out beyond the limits of our previous notions of engineering science into the complex and fascinating world of fractals. We can adapt their characteristics and potentials to the subject of our discourse: the factory *with* a future.

What we have so far thought and done was 'perfect', but let us now look for something better

The Fractal Factory is an integrating approach. In this, its multidimensionality comes to the fore. We are proud of our technology and organizations, but we have neglected or failed to sufficiently appreciate the human factor as the agent of these potentials. This has led us to treat companies as sterile objects. We have played this hand for what it was worth. What we need now is a 'new deal'.

It is no longer sufficient to correct existing structures and trouble-shooting is not the answer

The following definition summarizes the essential features of the new Fractal Factory as we understand it. Then we shall show what inferences for specific action can be derived from it.

We need new creative approaches born of changed thought patterns

Definition

A fractal is an independently acting corporate entity whose goals and performance can be precisely described.

- Fractals are self-similar; each one performs services.

Self-similarity

Self-organization

- Fractals practice self-organization:

    operatively: procedures are optimally organized by applying suitable methods.

Self-optimization

    tactically and strategically: fractals determine and formulate their goals in a dynamic process and decide upon internal and external contacts. Fractals restructure, regenerate and dissolve themselves.

Goal-orientation

- The system of goals that arises from the goals of the individual fractals is free from contradictions and must serve the objective of achieving corporate goals.

Dynamics

- Fractals are networked via an efficient information and communication system. They themselves determine the nature and extent of their access to data.

- The performance of a fractal is subject to constant assessment and evaluation.

We need a new corporate culture

The fractal thereby becomes the central structuring element in the company. To the uninformed visitor, however, the Fractal Factory will hardly be identifiable as such through external features. Rather, its potential lies in internal values, in the corporate culture, as we shall see later.

Our usual critical approach is reactive and often destroys creativity, our real strength

Here, the author is opening himself up to the criticism of confronting specialists with new terminology. A sense of insecurity has recently been aroused in this regard by the rapid creation and propagation of buzz words, which has had the fatal consequence of bringing about a tendency to reject all new approaches.

I still have a vivid recollection of the dismissive gesture made by an experienced production manager when one of these neologisms, most of which come from the Far East, cropped up in conversation. However, this penchant for rejecting the new is far from justified. Admittedly, scientific research must face the criticism that it does not always express itself in the language of the pragmatist, even when it wishes to address him directly, and that it does not always do justice to its prime objective: to think ahead.

Intelligent people are particularly prone to defending their behavior instead of listening

In spite of all this, this new expression is necessary because the Fractal Factory is not merely an extension of existing models, but requires a change in the self-image of all concerned. Any attempts to slavishly transfer the characteristics described below will simply not work. Above and beyond the general principles, each company must find its own way in accordance with its own specific requirements.

A common effort is required to replace present achievements with something better

The characteristic of self-similarity

The characteristic of self-similarity refers not only to the structural characteristics of organizational design. It circumscribes the manner of performing a service as well as the formulation and pursuance of goals. This makes it clear why the Fractal Factory *must* be an integrated approach. It is multidimensional.

Each individual must perform his task as comprehensively as the company

One of the essential requirements which we have stipulated for production structures with a future is the capacity for entrepreneurial ways of thinking and acting in all areas, right down to the individual employee. If the image that this conjures up of independently operating units is valid, then each fractal must itself be a (little)

Complexity forces us to distinguish the important from the unimportant and to act accordingly. Priorities change from day to day

'Fractal Factory'. And to a certain extent this is indeed the case. Self-*similarity* permits deviations. In fractal geometry, too, there exist only similar, never identical, structures.

Because of the variety of possible solutions to individual problems, fractals with identical goals and input and output variables can indeed have quite different internal structures (fig. 56).

The new challenge: internal and external network management

Furthermore, a fractal need not necessarily remain *in* the factory, but can become completely independent. In this way, a network of companies is created, all of which are closely interconnected and which we regard as fractals.

Centralized functions should be measured according to their contribution to the value-creation chain

Of course we can not entirely dispense with centralized functions in a Fractal Factory. For example, a central resource planning or planning support, which comes into operation temporarily as the need arises, and also the concentration of specialized knowledge which can not continuously be maintained in the fractals.

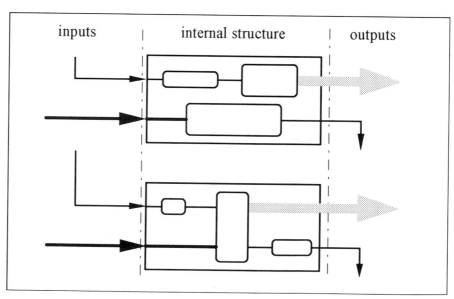

Fig. 56: Self-similar fractals

All support mechanisms concerning the organization are available to all fractals. In particular,
this refers to the availability of information,
which is no longer monopolized. Each fractal,
and this in the end means each workplace, must
be regarded in the same light as the whole
company. All services must be performed in
their entirety and all tasks completed as independently as possible. This involves quality,
quantity, economic use of resources, reliability
and speed. In the event that a fractal is not in a
position to achieve this independently, it will
seek help, ideally only for a limited period,
from 'outside', i.e. from other fractals. And
these can also offer, or take advantage of, for
example, a centralized service operation.
Initially, however, it must always be assumed
that tasks are performed in their entirety with
definite input and output variables.

*Information should
no longer be
monopolized, but
made generally
available*

*In the interests of
holistic task com-
pletion, externally
provided services
should be kept to a
minimum*

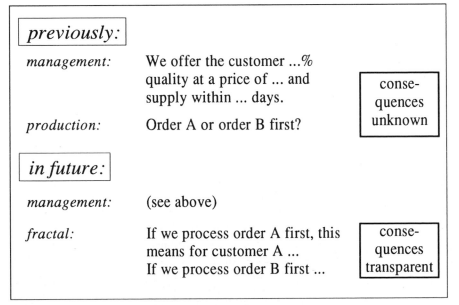

Fig. 57: Goal inheritance

The company's goals, like those of the fractals, are self-similar. They differ in detail and specific implementation

But it is by no means enough to create 'factories within a factory' if it can not be ensured that they are all pulling in the same direction. Unfortunately, hotly defended spheres of influence continue to be the rule rather than the exception in our business organizations.

But neither is it sufficient to create corporate models which can not be converted into daily practice. For this reason we use the term self-similarity to refer primarily to the goals of the company and its fractals. Global goals which have quite sensibly been formulated in general terms must be turned into specific action. In order for this to take place 'synchronously' in all fractals, their goals are formulated in much more concrete terms. For a machinist who enjoys a large degree of autonomy, for example, it is not immediately obvious what effects his decisions may have on the customer orientation of the company (fig. 57). Because the goals of all fractals are *similar*, it is in fact guaranteed that all individual activities can be blended together to form a harmonious whole. The central aspect of the goal-formation process is dealt with in a separate chapter.

The characteristic of self-organization

The process of constant improvement must be put into direct effect immediately

Self-organization in the Fractal Factory affects both the operative and the tactical and strategic levels. This means that good ideas, wherever they come from, can be implemented. The process of constant improvement takes direct and immediate effect and therefore continues to be a major force.

Operative self-organization means the application of suitable methods for controlling processes. These problems have already been mentioned in connection with production control (cf. p. 108). Of course - and this is precisely the strength of the Fractal Factory - different fractals also use different methods. Let us just take the following quite common example from practice: a company's best-selling line is manufactured in large quantities. At the same time an exclusive version is essential for reasons of image. This necessitates additional manufacturing operations and in particular involves a considerable amount of individual data processing. It is advisable to organize production as far as possible in a horizontal fashion, shared by two fractals.

Self-organization requires the freedom to use the methods appropriate to a particular task

The common practice in such cases, which can be observed again and again, is to increase the flexibility of the mass production system with a correspondingly detrimental decrease in overall cost-effectiveness. A Fractal Factory, however, welcomes the separation of mass-produced lines from more exotic ones. On the other hand it does not prevent the integration of both types of manufacture should appropriate technical solutions be available, e.g. by exploiting the potential of flexible manufacturing systems. There are already many examples of the initial stages of self-organizing systems being implemented in practice. A number of case studies are given below, starting with Hewlett-Packard's PCB plant in Böblingen:

The same method is often applied to perform quite different tasks, with the result that the overall cost-effectiveness of production falls

Self-organization has already found its way into shop-floor practice

"Each employee from the manager to the stock clerk understands that all processes in the company, whether decisions, actions or even inaction, influence each other through constant feedback. Effects become the causes of new effects, which in turn initiate still fur-

Minor disturbances can be blown up into disastrous events

Since setting priorities for complex situations is a subjective matter, problems must be solved, and action must be taken, where they arise

ther developments. The smallest defect can be multiplied and have disastrous consequences. Whoever asks about the cause of an effect, misunderstands the process. And these enigmatic interrelationships can only really be controlled in very narrow confines.

In this system the employees form a largely autonomous communication structure which they control and from which they are controlled... Their superiors no longer watched every move their staff were making, but specified tasks and goals in such a way 'that everybody knew what was important'.

The employees perform self-regulation, self-determination and self-administration in groups

For the 130 participants in the experiment, self-regulation ('how do we divide the work within the group?') and self-administration ('how do we deal with group members who do not keep to the rules?') have now become a matter of course."   [Manager Magazine 1991]

A further example shows that even (and especially) a 'product development' fractal can be given new life through the principle of self-organization:

In the R & D department, each research assistant is permitted to spend 15 % of his time on his own projects

'If the brainwaves do not dry up at 3M, then this is due to ... the innovative climate.' Each research assistant in the development department is permitted to spend 15 percent of his time on research projects of his own - without being called upon to account for his activities. If an employee needs funds for his own projects, for example for the acquisition of a special laboratory device, there is a fund of a million dollars per year available. (Its allocation is decided upon by a committee.) The self-adhesive 'post-it' memos which make 300 million dollars a year for 3M are the result of such an individual project. Furthermore, the management is expected to exercise 'considerable tolerance' in accordance with internal guidelines. 'After all ... innovating means risking something new, leaving the beaten track.' A further motto runs: 'employees make mistakes. But in the long term, the manager who runs his department in a dictatorial manner and believes that he has to prescribe exactly how each of his subordinates has to perform his task, is making a worse mistake.' And finally: 'it is better to beg forgiveness than to ask for permission.' [FAZ, September 27, 1991]

Innovating means leaving the beaten track

It is better to beg forgiveness than permission

In addition to operative self-organization, the strategic and tactical components also apply in the Fractal Factory. The aim is to achieve global objectives locally. The structuring process which is common today in a factory or a manufacturing system is always driven from outside. Such planning impetus usually arises only as a result of defects which can not be overlooked and therefore comes much too late. We must understand that not only the procedures, but also the processes of structure formation require powerful dynamics in order to do justice to changing demands. We call this process dynamic structuring.

Structural design must also be driven from within and demands a highly dynamic approach

The characteristics of dynamics and vitality

The Fractal Factory is not the first structuring approach. We have already referred to the traditional notion of manufacturing segmentation and to its decisive weakness: its static nature. We expect more from a fractal than we do from a segment, a manufacturing island, or whatever

Vitality is the ability to act successfully under changing environmental influences

the basic unit of structure may be called. A fractal must have the decisive characteristic of *vitality*.

Speed of response is essential

The term vitality, drawn from the field of biology or medicine, denotes the 'power to sustain life', the 'life force' or simply 'liveliness'. Originally only applied to living things, this term can also be used to describe a similar characteristic in intelligent systems, systems which adapt and react to the influences of their respective environments. In this sense the expression has often been used in recent times to refer to business enterprises. This vision is based on a rejection of a one-dimensional view dominated by balance-sheet ratios, profit and loss accounts and liquidity ratios. The vitality of a company can be observed over time, whereby several 'stages of life' can be distinguished: conception - realization - maturity - optimization - aging and overaging.

Financial statistics say nothing about vitality

Market saturation only means that no innovation has taken place in the product range

Insufficient vitality in a company always ends in stagnating or falling profits, lost market shares and a loss of competitiveness. It is therefore one of the prime tasks to constantly adapt the company or its structure to currrent demands.

Influence on vitality is exercised by internal success factors, for example:

Vitality means constantly discovering and taking advantage of success factors

- cost situation
- manufacturing potential
- research and development
- management efficiency
- purchasing and distribution potential
- financial potential
- logistics
- location
- staff
- manufacturing range or product program

as well as by external environmental success factors such as

- outlet markets
- supply markets
- competition
- legislation.

The knowledge and abilities proffered must provide benefits by catering for needs

If we may risk a comparison from the world of biology: however well the bodily functions are organized and coordinated, a diseased organ can - depending on the severity of the disease - restrict or even prevent the functioning of the whole system.

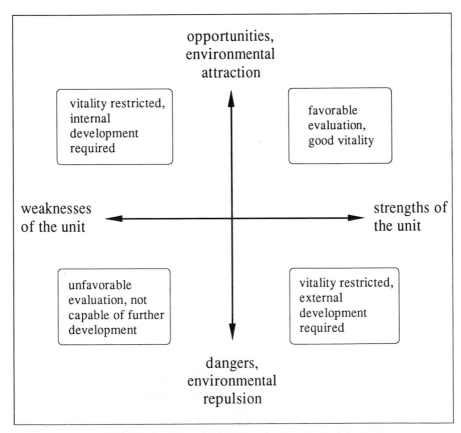

Fig. 58: Positions within the vitality ratio portfolio

The goal: forms of organization in which vital elements, the fractals, largely structure themselves and together serve the whole system

Two factors are decisive for the vitality of the fractal: the strengths of the unit (abilities, skills) and the corresponding requirements which are to be met by this fractal. Fig. 58 shows possible positions in just such a ratio portfolio.

In the description of the natural processes of structure formation we referred to the principle of regulating parameters which 'mysteriously' control the global behavior of individual and independent system elements. It is still a puzzle to us how nature manages to combine so many constantly changing elements in such a way as to produce a system that is immune to disruptive external influences. But it is precisely this that we should aim for in our factory with a future: independent, vital elements which form themselves into groups even in the absence of external pressure in the interests of serving the whole company.

Dynamic structuring is based above all on interaction between fractals

The mechanism of dynamic structuring is based largely on an analysis of the interrelationships within and between fractals. These relationships have quite distinct features. Fig. 59 shows the

relational layer	*features (typical)*
hierarchical level	authority to direct
data processing level	work schedules
informal level	personal contacts
physical level	material flow
sociological level	emotions
technological level	information transfer
financial level	rates of pay

Fig. 59: Relational layers in the Fractal Factory

criteria according to which they may be structured. It is easy to see that the field of view has been considerably extended when compared to traditional structuring approaches.

As regards system theory, fractals should be formed in such a way that relationships (flow of material, staff and information) within the fractal are stronger than those to the outside. If this ceases to be the case, then it is advisable to adapt the structures accordingly (fig. 60). For example, a structural adaptation is required if possibilities for process integration are opened up as a result of new developments in technology.

Fractal formation: the internal relationships within a fractal are closer and more intensive than those to the outside

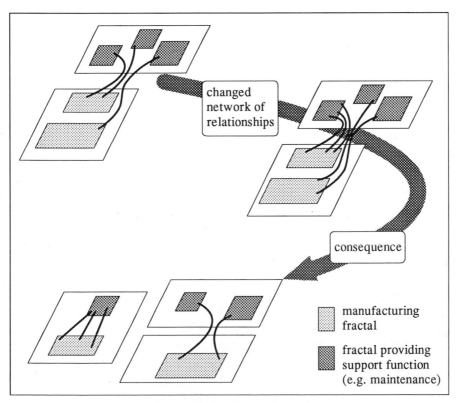

Fig. 60: Dynamic restructuring of a manufacturing area

The idea of forming decentralized business units or segregating functions which are not part of the core business is familiar. But mostly a rigid organization remains

The formation of reasonably small corporate units is a promising approach enabling rapid reaction to market changes. In an extreme case this leads to legal independence, in other words the organizational dissolution of company ties. In practice this can be observed amongst large conglomerates which have been formed as a result of diversification or acquisitions. If we change to decentralized organizational and management principles, then this is the only way to put a concern which is no-longer manageable back on the road to success. On the one hand this approach is quite radical, but on the other hand it usually stops at the factory gate. The problems of interaction between the corporate functions involved are not solved, only reduced to more manageable proportions.

There are a variety of regulating criteria for structure formation

Within a company there are a number of different regulating critera for structure formation. The following may be regarded as the main ones:

- product
- procedures and materials
- information and communication requirements
- material flow
- staff
- learning and experience requirements

In the future there will continue to be a variety of structures and of very differently organized factories

Consistent, successive application of these aspects points us towards familiar structures. Concentrating on materials and processes, for example, leads us to classical workshop production, in which similar activities are grouped together to facilitate the accumulation of knowledge and experience. The application of cost degression via mass production on the other hand takes the product as its regulating criterion. The whole factory structure is tailored to this product. Both staff-orientation and task-orientation can result in the formation of production islands or segments. In this, the regulating structure can be clearly seen in the physical arrangement of operational areas. In addition, competences and chains of communications are determined at the same time.

It has surely not escaped the reader that we are now on familiar territory. The previous remarks could be used to justify traditional structural approaches. The main difference lies in the recognition of a changed field of action and changed goals. Here, classical methods do not help. But the Fractal Factory does.

The search for the right structure can only partly be objective. This does not mean that aids or methods for organizational design do not exist. For example, a cluster analysis can be

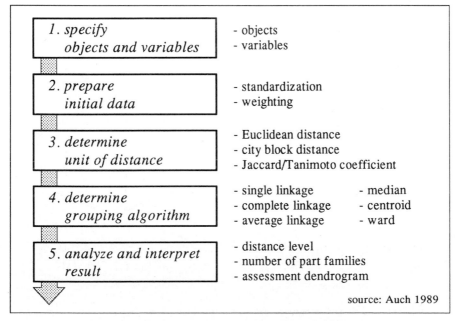

Fig. 61: Flow chart of a cluster analysis

The structuring process can only be partly objective. One kind of aid is the cluster analysis which illustrates the degree of relationship

used to systematically analyze the elements for similarities (fig. 61). But model formation itself, i.e. defining and quantifying characteristics, involves a considerable simplification of the nature of the problem. Furthermore the scaling, that is, the weighting accorded to the various characteristics, has a decisive influence on the result.

The result of a cluster analysis is effected by the weighting of the characteristics

This effect is all too often concealed when a process is implemented on a computer. Users without knowledge of methods and computing are in danger of accepting the result as being objectively 'right'. And once again we find ouselves confronted with the phenomenon of the deterministic view of the world. The problem of structural design can not, in all its complexity, be reduced to an algorithm. Even if the

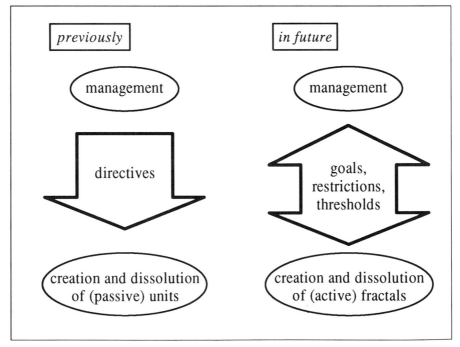

Fig. 62: Creation and dissolution of fractals

ultimate solution *were* to be found, we could not exclude the possibility of it being merely a relative optimum which is valid only for a short time.

The result is only valid for a short time

Practice has shown that in the majority of cases the product, or rather the task of production, provides a promising design approach. Against this background, the process of segmentation which we have already discussed may be justified as a practical method. First, vertical segments are formed within which 'substructures' can subsequently develop. This provides the practician with easy-to-use rules of action which in most cases produce tangible improvements.

The manufacturing task is usually a good place to start the process of organizational design, but this can preclude a comprehensive solution

A comprehensive approach such as the Fractal Factory avoids emphasis on the product as the prime factor, since this would preclude a whole range of solutions at the outset. Factories whose prime resource resides in the skills of their workforce will do well to base their external and internal structures on this aspect. In other cases, it would not make sense to duplicate

segments / factories within the factory	*fractals*
- manufacture - are structured once only, at a specific point in time (impetus from outside) - are suitable for a stable environment - work according to specified goals - are self-responsible - are assessed according to results	- perform services (in the widest - sense) are subject to a constant process of change (dynamic structuring) - are suitable for a turbulent environment - are integrated into the goal-formation process - organize and administer themselves - navigate

Fig. 63: Comparison of fractals and segments

particularly expensive plant or machinery purely for the sake of segmentation.

All participants are expected to act as service providers and to think in terms of the market

The relationship between fractals is based on the provision of services. Fractals must be able to withstand internal and external competition, since each one has the option of entering into alternative relationships in the interests of performing its task as a whole. This demands free market thinking on the part of all concerned. The creation and dissolution of elements is a further feature of vital structures (fig. 62).

Fig. 63 summarizes the differences between fractals and segments. The notion of navigation referred to there will be dealt with in more detail later.

An old rule: simplify and maintain order

The task: to integrate a multitude of diverse aspects

With the Fractal Factory we are confronted with the task of integrating a multiplicity of diverse aspects. This can only succeed as long as we maintain an overall view, otherwise we find ourselves poking about in the dark with no real idea of how to create order from chaos. A familiar situation will help to illustrate this:

Very few of today's computer users can say very much about the insides of their 'machine'. Nor is this normally necessary; all that matters is the result. A good many contemporaries can still remember the long and laborious manual calculations that used to be necessary. Later it was possible to enlist the aid of computer systems which amazed many people but required a deep insight into their internal workings.

The path to the solution always takes us from the primitive via the complicated to the simple

This observation reflects a development which can be experienced in many areas of engineering. When a new problem is being solved, the development path proceeds from the *primitive* via the *complicated* to the *simple.*

Simplification reduces the amount of learning and teaching involved, since the quantity of information to be assimilated, processed and stored is reduced. Today 'simple' means that the user of an 'tool', which can be a camera, a photocopier, an automobile, a machine tool or a computer, can concentrate on performing his task, e.g. his actual manufacturing task and not on operating his 'tool'. The inevitable result of this is a 'dequalification' of the user. Internally, though, the products become more and more complex, and this affects the supplier, since the amount of development work increases.

Simple means user-friendly and task-oriented

Seen in this light, the full potential of data processing systems is not yet being adequately and consistently exploited. Often, the user only utilizes those functions which he requires repeatedly, in most cases far fewer than the number installed.

User-friendly products must de-qualify, whereby internal complexity and development work increases

We must strive for 'simple' solutions in all areas, but all too often we still find ourselves in the 'complicated' or even 'primitive' stage. It is a serious mistake to misuse ever-more efficient data processing systems to solve problems that have remained too complex. The effort required to achieve this makes it an uneconomical proposition. This of course also goes for the Fractal Factory. Without simplification we would never be in a position to identify the totality, let alone improve it. It is not Sisyphus who provides us with a model, but Mandelbrot, who reduced insuperable complexity to simple iterations.

It is a mistake to misuse the effi-ciency of data processing systems to control processes which are too complicated

First simplification, then automation; this means reducing the amount of information processing

An old rule: first simplify, then automate

Man is still the most efficient processor of information and knowledge

The rule, "maintain order" reduces information processing to a minimum and makes cost-effective auto-mation possible

required to perform a manufacturing task to a minimum. As humans, i.e. from the point of view of the most efficient 'knowledge processing machine' there is, we are not aware of the amount of information processing that takes place when we are working. But the nature of the matter becomes apparent when we want to hand over a task to a robot. Complicated sensors (tactile, optical and acoustic) are required and the programming itself is not exactly simple, either. The cost of the engineering work involved is often prohibitive. For this reason products and process must first be simplified, i.e. designed to facilitate manufacture and assembly.

If we maintain order in the production process, for example by avoiding 'reaching into a box of jumbled up workpieces', then we similarly reduce the amount of information processing required for an economical solution. A crass example of this is the success of worldwide container transport. The increase in speed and productivity which could be achieved justified investment in containers, new ships, new docks equipment and vehicles. The amount of information processing at the transport interfaces

---

Maintaining order throughout:
- production unit
  = transport unit/conveyor unit
  = warehouse unit/storage system
  = feed unit/ordering system
  = assembly unit
- automatic handling at material flow interfaces

Fig. 64: Design of material flow and transport chain

was reduced to a minimum. Whereas a conventional freighter could be loaded with goods such as crates, sacks and barrels at the rate of 5 t per man and shift, a dockworker can reach a container-turnover of 200 t per shift, which corresponds to a 40-fold increase in productivity.

So the rule stated above is based on the following directive: reduce the information processing required to perform the production task to an absolute minimum, and only then develop a technical solution. It is a fundamental requirement of the Fractal Factory that the principle of 'simplicity' be implemented across the whole breadth of the company. Whereas this maxim is being observed in some subdivisions, there is still a long way to go as far as organizational development is concerned. In order to enable really adequate structural design, precise target states must be known, which of course in the case of the Fractal Factory is not a state at all, but rather a dynamic process.

We must implement the principle of "simplicity" throughout the whole company

Communication and information

As we have already indicated on a number of occasions, in the Fractal Factory information processing assumes a special significance. However, it must never be allowed to become an end in itself, which is currently all too often the case.

Computer integration must be examined for feasibility and cost-effectiveness

Whenever we have discussed the factory of the future in recent years, our model has been based on a factory resembling a complex machine, which advances in information technology will sooner or later have enabled us to automate. Starting from automated material processing, universal communication and

The CIM approach is function and data oriented. The expense of implementation can only be borne once, resulting in rigid, obsolete structures

information systems designed to ensure shorter reaction times with low stock levels were developed and even partly implemented. Such a universal concept is referred to as "computer integrated manufacturing" (CIM). Today's CIM components are based on the dialectics of a function and data oriented view [Scheer 1990]. An integrated CIM concept can therefore only be developed for all functional areas simultaneously. The tremendous expense which this necessitates can only be borne once and this therefore results in rigid hierarchical system structures, which are characterized by innumerable interfaces between the system components. This state of affairs is illustrated in Fig. 65 which depicts the external and internal information flows within a corporation.

Structures must not be cemented; the connection between organization and information structures must be examined

It is often wrongly assumed that the organizational structure and the procedures of a company can automatically be improved by the implementation of these computer aided information systems. This is a fallacy. It is more likely to lead to the cementation of the existing procedures and structures of the company in question than to their improvement. The costs of modification and constant improvement of procedures remain prohibitive for the foreseeable future. In order to avoid this, it is now often advocated that an analysis and optimization of corporate procedures and structures should take place before CIM is introduced. In the short term this approach may indeed seem to facilitate an optimized implementation of a CIM system. However, this method only depicts the optimum structure at the time of implementation. Today's CIM components provide no support for the modifications of procedures and structures which may be required to meet changing exter-

First analysis, then integration; are the structures still ideal?

nal and internal factors of influence. This can be
clearly seen from the example of PPS systems.
Because of the permanently predefined scheduling algorithms used to initiate manufacturing
jobs, a comprehensive modification of the
manufacturing process to changed conditions
(e.g. a change from mass-production to batch
production) is not possible.

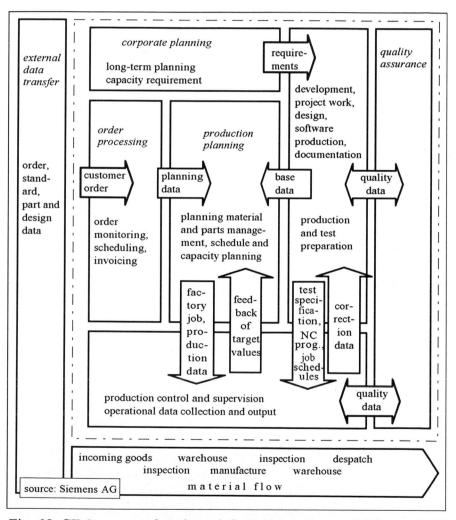

Fig. 65: CIM concept: functions, information and material flow within
a factory (mass production)

CIM must become a tool for high-speed communication

In the Fractal Factory cooperation between the self-regulating and self-organizing factory fractals is characterized by high individual dynamics and maximum ability to react to dynamically changing conditions. In order to determine the vitality of the individual factory fractals, it is necessary to perform continuous assessment through comparison with competitors. At this point it becomes clear that even the traditional notion of CIM, at least in its strictest sense as a purely technical means of intergrating computerized factory islands, becomes suspect. Seen from this rather narrow perspective, when CIM is implemented in a Fractal Factory, it can only fulfil a subordinate function as a tool. The CIM systems of the future, on the other hand, will have an important task. They must provide flexible and efficient information and *navigation systems* for the fractals of a factory. Information systems have the task of providing the data required for the manufacture of products and the allocation of operating resources within the framework of a suitable manufacturing process. New navigation systems should be designed to support the independently operating continuous efficiency improvement processes of fractals. This requirement is of central importance since in future only global company goals will be set by the management system and these must be converted into action at the local level. Instead of continuing to carry out ever more detailed monitoring with the aid of CIM systems, the Fractal Factory will only conduct a result-oriented assessment of a fractal. The relevant organizational structures will be continuously optimized and adapted by each individual fractal in the light of any changes that may occur.

Fractals need information for their tasks and navigational systems for paths and goals

Evaluation is based on results. The benefit must justify the effort involved

Current developments in CIM do not yet fully do justice to this when measured by the standards required for their implementation within the framework of a Fractal Factory. An important goal that must be pursued throughout the world is the comprehensive modelling of data and functions integrating all static and dynamic interrelations of a factory in order to make them available to an optimized computer aided system. The high costs of one-off special applications of CIM should be reduced through standardization (fig. 66). Over the years, this work has given rise to an insight which leads away from the rigid structures of data and operation based methods towards object-oriented approaches. If we refer to the 'object' of a model language as the 'fractal of information technology', then it is easy to see how this relates to the context of the Fractal Factory. Fundamental tools for a comprehensive communication and

The required standardization of interfaces leads us from a concentration on data and functions to an object-oriented view

In addition to communication and information systems, we must develop navigation systems so that fractals can optimize themselves

graphics	GKS-3-D	graphical kernel system (ISO)
	CGI	computer graphics interface (ISO)
	CGM	computer graphics metafile (ISO)
	PHIGS	programmers hierarchical graphics system (ISO)
drawings, geometry	IGES	initial graphics exchange specification (ANSI)
	SET	standard d'échange et de transport (AFNOR)
	VDAFS	VDA surface interface (DIN)
product models	PDES	product data exchange specifications (NBS)
	STEP	standard for exchange of product model data (ISO)
	CAD-NT	CAD standard parts
machine controls	IRDATA	industrial robot data
	APT	automatically programmed tools (ISO)
	CLDATA	cutter location data (ISO)
protocols	MAP	manufacturing automation protocol (ISO)
	TOP	technical and office protocol

source: DIN

Fig. 66: International standards

information system are created by establishing basic models, but navigation systems are not yet in evidence in any work currently in progress. It is therefore desirable that further developments in CIM, which will extend beyond the basic functions we have mentioned, should take into account the perspectives and requirements of implementing CIM in a Fractal Factory.

The future of CIM involves network management. Information is generated, stored, updated and responded to in many places. Mutual access is provided for

The mutual dependencies and influences amongst the structures of fractal organizations and systems will not make it any easier to design a CIM environment. On the one hand a much higher degree of autonomy, and therefore intelligence, is required in the computer aided fractals. On the other hand it is necessary to provide an efficient decentralized navigation and information system. The increasing independence and competence of employees in turn requires a greater willingness to accept added responsibility and correspondingly enhanced skills on the part of all employees. In a Fractal Factory, therefore, particular significance must be attached to the following points:

The most intensive communication takes place within the fractal, between humans and computers; this relieves the network

- model language paradigms e.g. object-oriented and agent concepts which support the systematic aspects of fractal thinking
- user openness and transparency in CIM systems
- expert-system supported information gathering and compression
- provision for evaluation via simulation prior to the execution of expensive operations

We must develop our own concepts for CIM and set the course accordingly

- knowledge-based process scheduling, execution and control systems
- intelligent control mechanisms providing short feedback loops between decision maker and real process

If CIM is regarded as an information and communication tool, it can make a significant contribution to the success of a Fractal Factory.

Telecommunications are without doubt one of the greatest boom areas worldwide. In Europe it already accounts for about 3.5 percent of GDP and according to an EC study this will double in the next few years. The keen interest shown by industry in taking a share of the market for digital mobile telephone systems, for example, is an impressive indication of the expectations aroused by this trend. Technological leaps in the fields of

Efficient and economical telecommunications between fractals is of major importance

- digital technology
- mobile telecommunications and
- broadband networks

open up new applications which are also of great importance to the process of providing industrial services. Data transfer links with suppliers are already commonplace in many com-

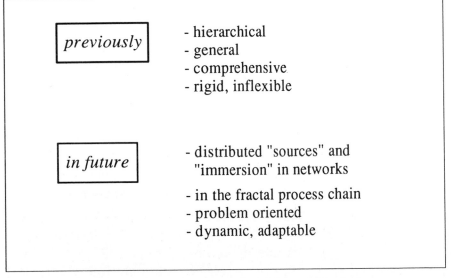

Fig. 67: Information systems today and in future

panies. Indeed, in most just-in-time concepts they are a precondition for a well-organized factory. Satellite communication and navigation systems now even make it possible to determine the location of a vehicle to within a few meters and to display the position at the command center.

Traffic problems limit the use of just-in-time concepts. Their value to the economy is doubtful

However, this only temporarily alleviates such traffic problems as tailbacks and it is precisely this situation which pushes many JIT concepts onto the sidelines. Consequently, as we have already discussed in the section on future visions, a factory can be 'dislocated', so that the physical production of goods is performed as closely as possible to the place of consumption. Once the transmission of data and of verbal and visual communication over long distances no longer represents a barrier, it is conceivable that a workpiece can be developed in Europe and put into production immediately in another continent in a service center incorporated into a worldwide manufacturing network. Even if this vision still begs many questions, it should nevertheless provide a good deal of food for thought, since decentralized autonomous structures are conducive to just such physical segregation.

Telecommunications opens the way for decentralized, autonomous and physically separated units, for which we use the term fractal

However, there is still a long way to go here. Experience with screen-based workplaces which have been transposed into the homes of employees can hardly provide a successful model since they completely ignore the motivational aspect of community experience.

Transcontinental videoconferencing on the other hand is enjoying increasing popularity because it combines time and cost savings. Even if it is no substitute for a personal meeting, it is a welcome resource which is much appreciated in times of international crisis (e.g. in the spring of 1991).

Of course there are considerable development gaps in this area, in particular in terms of data formats and interfaces. But on the other hand work on these aspects is proceeding apace and the dynamics of this market are sure to lead to a rapid fall in prices with a corresponding increase in their availability, as was the case with microelectronics in the eighties.

There will be a progressive increase in the use of internal and external telecommuni-cations

Goal-formation processes

So how do fractals obtain the main controlling variables required for the Fractal Factory - their goals? It should be obvious that these can not be imposed upon them, since they then could not possibly serve their purpose. It seems to be more appropriate to generate them in a process of coordination between the participating fractals and to modify them as necessary. This is supported by an inheritance mechanism which ensures the consistency of the goal system:

Goal-formation: a process of coordi-nation

The goal system arrived at through coordination with the level immediately superior to it is supplemented by each fractal according to considerations of expediency, for the closer the task is to the manufacturing process, the more specific the goal system must be. Each fractal therefore has an individual and consistent system of current goals. Consistency is guaranteed because any contradiction can be identified immediately.

Each fractal must have a coordi-nated, individual, current and consis-tent system of goals

Methods of management that are based primarily on prescribing goals and carrying out subsequent checks have commonly come to be

Management by objectives was an important development in management methodology; it is also applicable to fractals

termed 'management by objectives'. They represent an important milestone on the long path of organizational development because they leave the person concerned free to map out his own route to achieving the goals.

However, the idea of relinquishing competence beyond operative activities goes against the grain of almost all company executives. But on the basis of daily experience in the institute that I run, I can attest that this need not be the case. In view of the exponential increase in knowledge that has taken place, I can no longer pursue all aspects of the subjects covered. Incidentally, this development can also be observed in more general areas: where it used to be a matter of course for a foreman to be able to perform all activities within the scope of his responsibility, (and often he was best at them) this is now coming to apply less and less.

Senior management must develop a new self-image

Competent staff need freedom of action

Because my assistants enjoy a greater specialized competence in their own particular fields (otherwise they would be in the wrong place) it is advisable to grant them correspondingly more freedom of decision, which extends far beyond the operative level. Decisions to enter or leave new spheres of activity can indeed be made by the persons concerned - through the acquisition of research and development projects supported by private enterprise or public bodies.

A shallow hierarchical order and structure will still be necessary in order to give each team member a "home" in a social environment

This system has proved itself because it conforms to the requirements of the market for R & D knowledge and expertise. Working parties grow and shrink and a diffusion into other areas of knowledge takes place, guaranteeing that the results are closely related to practical applications. Of course, at this point the objection may be raised that this is taking place under almost 'clinical' conditions, since the members of a scientific team have an immediate interest in working on future-oriented and rewarding projects. But in spite of this, the basic notion surely remains transferable. What is more, this principle does not contradict the idea of a hierarchical arrangement; at my institute there are - perhaps I should say, still - five levels of hierarchy, in which each member has his place, his 'home', as it were, in the social environment.

Let us examine somewhat more closely the process for formulating goals in the example in question: each research assistant has the goal of obtaining further qualifications after his examination and of expressing his work in the form of a thesis. In the first place this is a very private, one might almost say selfish, goal. In order to attain it he needs a suitable intellectual environment, appropriate facilities and last but not least, material security. In addition to this he will wish for a good social climate in his working environment to promote a positive mental attitude.

The activities of the institute are to no small degree financed through R & D projects carried out for industry. The more personal interests and projects worked on have in common, the greater the advantage is for the individual. Furthermore, he has an interest in acquiring a qualification for which there is a corresponding demand, since this increases his own market value. Of course, there are many more aspects to this matter, but let us summarize the main points:

The members of a fractal influence the creation and dissolution of knowledge

The subject and content of a dissertation arise from an iterative process. By publishing his work, a research assistant makes a name for himself in his chosen field, which leads to corresponding customer enquiries and - hopefully - to further projects.

It is obvious from this that the individual thereby influences the direction taken by the development of his subject group. On the other hand, the same mechanism ensures that obsolete specialist knowledge for which there is no longer a demand is dispensed with. This effect is accelerated still further by the high turnover of assistants, who as a rule only remain at the institute for a limited time and then take their knowledge with them - in the positive sense of a rapid and effective transfer of technology.

Most members have a good feeling for opportunities and risks

Experience shows that there is a very good feeling for opportunities and risks at this 'lower' level. Of course, neither the individual nor his team of specialists operate in a vacuum, but engage in dialog with their superiors. But it has been demonstrated time and time again that the superiors' tasks consist mainly in providing support and advice and in making things easier.

The most important task for superiors: support, advice and general assistance

Of course it is inevitable that technical restrictions of various kinds force decisions which are not always to the liking of the persons concerned. But in principle we can say:

- The goal-formation process involves all persons concerned.

The goal-formation process must include all participants; it is a control loop

- This process has the character of a control loop incorporating all relevant parameters (market requirements, technical restrictions such as financing and individual moral concepts).
- The organization continues to develop autonomously.

At the expense of exaggeration, one could claim that as far as the latter point is concerned, even strategic developments are governed from 'below'. This effect can be observed in practice: the institute's directors regularly carry out organizational modifications (e.g. formation or merging of groups), but with hindsight the origins of these changes can be traced back to gradual developments which in many cases could not be seen 'from above'.

Organizational design is often directed or imposed "from below"

If we begin by defining the global goal of the institute as the desire to provide significant contributions to applied research and development in manufacturing technology, then the goals pursued in each fractal down to the individual employee assume their place within this system, and the inheritance mechanism is evident in its full force.

Of course there are also central functions in the IPA, such as the library, communications service - formerly the data processing centre - and administration. The alert reader will see that this does not contradict the idea of a fractal organization. These are service functions which are centrally organized, since they are used by everybody.

The value-creating units will continue to require central services in the future, but these can also be regarded as measurable fractals

As a final indication of the fractal character of the institute I would like to point to the establishment some ten years ago of the Fraunhofer Institute for Industrial Engineering, which grew out of one of the main departments of the IPA, since its sphere of operations and the size of the department made the formation of an independent unit advisable. If we regard the Fraunhofer Society as a blanket organization, then many characteristics can be observed which are indicative of a fractal organization. Furthermore, the Society's institutions are often restructured or closed down as their fields of attention become obsolete.

Of course a decentralized fractal organization also has its problems, such as duplication, which must be taken into account

From all this, in particular in view of the fact that these institutions have to assert themselves in the marketplace, I think I can safely conclude that there are structures to be found here which can be transferred to other organizations.

When we speak of goals, then we basically mean systems of goals. As an example we can consider the classic state of conflict which exists between exploiting capacity, reducing inventories and minimizing the operating cycle. Such contradictions must be expressed and solved within the system of goals. This then gives us a goal profile which may include the definition of priorities.

We are faced with conflicting goals, which must be made transparent

The goal-formation mechanism described above is currently being used, at least to some extent, in industry. Goals developed independently by a given division are discussed with superiors and, after any necessary modifications have been made, are implemented. The results are positive, especially as far as producing a consistent system of goals is concerned. However, we must beware of the psychological pressure which may lead to performance goals being set which are too high. The unholy and partly grotesque experiences with 'self-commitment' in planned economies are adequate warning. Applied in appropriate measure, however, the goal-formation process is a reliable way of revealing any conflicts between competing goals, which in itself is of inestimable value.

The goal-formation process must continue to support self-commitment

Fig. 68 shows the goal-formation process. It is clear from this that even the personal goals of the employees can point in different directions.

The most familiar example is the conflict between the desire for more free time and that for a higher income. This conflict should be solved in the short term within the existing framework of goals (wage settlements, corporate agreements), but in the long term important personal goals can also influence this goal framework and cause it to shift. In the example we have just mentioned this has indeed happened in recent years. The wave of new schemes of working hours which resulted will in turn have consequences for the organizational structure.

Each individual is constantly faced with conflicting goals; this applies even more to an organization

Despite all the advantages which an iterative goal-formation process offers, it ties up resources and - this is very important - it can not be initiated by decree. And there must surely be cases in which it can not be implemented at all.

Even if the goal-formation process described is too extravagant, goal specification and monitoring can not be avoided in future

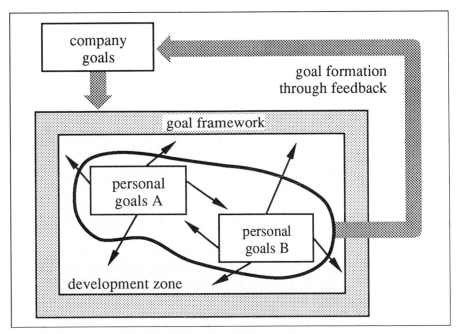

Fig. 68: The goal-formation process

So it will not be possible to dispense entirely with unidirectional specification and checking of goals. Nevertheless, this too, has its justification in the principle of ensuring a variety of possible solutions.

In a survey carried out by the American carpet industry the effects of various coordination instruments were analyzed:

Regular meetings and project groups generate mutual understanding

"Through regular personal meetings or common project groups, understanding of the other side was improved. The activity of specifying and monitoring goals corresponded to the desire of executives to manage strategically. After all, the use of planning procedures such as market studies developed individual strategic thinking in operative managers. Straightforward decisions by superiors and individual interface coordinators proved to be ineffective instruments of coordination. Furthermore, it was shown that the more intense interdepartmental planning becomes, the greater is the consensus when determining what priorities are necessary and what measures must be taken. This consensus between departments benefits the company, since specifying objectives and selecting methods through consensus between marketing and production lends the company a high market image. This was borne out by an independent assessment of manufacturers by wholesalers."
[Blick durch die Wirtschaft, Jan 2, 1992]

Harmony creates synergy effects

The Fractal Factory therefore demands a good measure of harmony. As the example shows, harmonized enterprises profit from additional synergy effects.

Navigation and control

In order to direct the 'movements' of the fractals within the whole process in the direction appropriate to each case, a function is needed, for which we have introduced the nautical metaphor of navigation. Fractals navigate in the sense that they are constantly checking their position within the target area, reporting it back and correcting it if necessary.

A further analogy - between medicine and business - would be justified, for even companies which have gotten into difficulties are kept alive for short periods of time by being fed considerable resources from outside in a process we could compare to a blood transfusion. However, this only takes place if there is a good prospect of full functionality being restored or if it is necessary to cushion the social impact.

In the section on approaches to organizational design current in Japan we encountered the term 'bionic manufacturing'. This approach favors a total decentralization of corporate functions. The company's main function is that of a blanket organization to provide a legal and financial framework. In this model the elements can also take up their positions on the free market but communicate closely with each other via computer links.

This notion must be treated with some scepticism. A factory can not be divided at will into viable units after the fashion of an amoeba. It is more appropriate to use the model of highly organized forms of life which, without central coordination, are unable to perform meaningful actions and therefore quickly succumb. However, by using a large amount of equipment it is possible to keep decentral organs, such as heart

Central coordination must govern the actions of decentralized units

and lungs, artificially alive even when the brain is not functioning.

Controlling is a management instrument used to coordinate activities

The strategic direction and management of a company can not be left to chance. The task derived from this fact is generally referred to as *controlling*. The term comes from the verb 'to control', used in the sense of a 'cybernetic, coordinating control of corporate activities' [Huch 1992].

The strategic direction of the company is determined by a few. Divisional objectives are the result of an iterative process of coordination

A participatory management system with a large degree of delegation of responsibility such as we encounter in the Fractal Factory requires - and we must not forget this - more advanced methods and instruments. As we have seen in the section on goal formation, many decision processes take place in a mixed top-down/bottom-up planning system; top-down and bottom-up approaches are combined and the strategic direction of the company is largely determined centrally by a small number of persons. The breakdown of this into departmental or divisional goals then follows in an iterative process of coordination. The goals and objectives thus formulated must not, however, be limited to budgetary consider-ations, but must also permit the use of other quantifiable variables.

Goal-formation and navigation are not a substitute for leadership, the "captain", but are more of an "able-bodied crew"

A variety of nested and interlocking control loops are at work in a com-pany

Within permitted limits, planning and control-ling is carried out in a bottom-up process. However, if the limits are overstepped, then the principle of 'management by exception' is applied. This enables mistakes to be prevented and corrected. The result is a variety of nested and interlocking control loops. Of course, these can not be formulated completely, since not all dependencies can be quantified, as is shown in the following inductive proof:

Let us assume that all control loops and their links were to be known. Then formal mathematical methods could be used to reduce the overall structure to a single, even if somewhat complex, formula. This would be the dream of all determinists, whereby we would have arrived at Chapter 3. Moreover it should be obvious that even the control loops are subject to a constant process of change.

Control loops can not be fully formulated nor quantified

In a Fractal Factory controlling has many more aspects than in traditional forms of organization. It is necessary to distinguish between the two aspects of data and methods. Data is made available throughout the whole company, whereas the question of physical storage is secondary and is determined by practical considerations. Access to this data and its processing require very advanced applications software, which must become much more user-friendly, since it will be used by all as a matter of course and will no longer be the preserve of the specialist. When information is condensed, a high priority must be accorded to consistency.

It is important to ensure constant availability of data and information; access and processing must become more user-friendly

We must overcome current difficulties with the interfaces between data and the processing software, since only a well-operating system will find the required acceptance. Fractals have access to a method kit which enables them to find solutions to the wide variety of short-term questions that can often arise. This kit should be under constant development.

Only a functioning system meets with acceptance at the operating level

In order to provide support for continuous structuring processes, fractals require suitable navigation and control instruments to

- determine their position and
- direct their continued development.

Navigation and control instruments for the fractals should be developed beyond existing methods. At the present time, the amount of preparation required is excessive

If we return to the example of structural development at my institute, we can identify such instrumentation; market demands can be identified through direct contact to industry. Any potentials which arise from extending technical facilities in the foreseeable future, and which seem to recommend corresponding preliminary measures, are the result of intensive and informed discussions combined with a study of specialist publications. The financial arrangements of the working party is determined by budgetary planning.

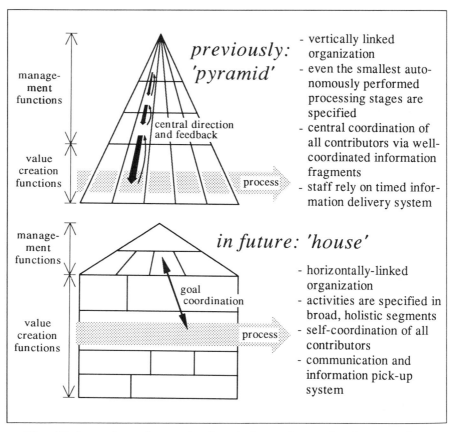

Fig. 69: Interplay of organization, information and value creation: from the pyramid to the house

At the moment the acquisition and assessment of this information is quite a wearisome process, since the multiplicity of information sources and data formats necessitate a great deal of preparation. There are absolutely no aids available for analyzing the informal level of system relationships. It is therefore especially important to develop suitable tools:

"... IBM intends to implement a new strategic concept in order to set the course for the integration of heterogeneous computer networks of any size in the nineties. 'Advanced peer-to-peer networking' (APPN) contains algorithms which are designed to enable participants to be sought and located anywhere in the network. In the event of enquiries from other systems, their previously unknown addresses are recognized and the knowledge is stored in directories and topological databases. In addition to defining its own location within the network and automatically locating all computers and terminals integrated into the network, APPN automatically finds the fastest path to each respective participant.

Information technology will provide open communications networks. Information and computer support are divorced from the organizational structure

The introduction of APPN will greatly simplify both installation and use of workstation computers and larger systems within the system network. It will enable equal (i.e. non-hierarchical) communication for the purposes of data and software exchange as well as the exploitation of data processing capacity independently of one's location in the network.

Other manufacturers' networks can be included in the existing worldwide IBM network by virtue of the open specifications of the IBM network access nodes."
    [Blick durch die Wirtschaft, April 6, 1992]

Management and the workforce

We began our deliberations by referring to the importance of humans in the Fractal Factory. Whereas they are seen from this perspective as the bearers of hope, they are regarded from other viewpoints more as obstacles, which in the past has led to attempts to treat them as a potentially disruptive factor and to eliminate them as much as possible through automation.

The vision of the Fractal Factory is based on today's notion of the workforce and their changing needs. Or is it true that workers are obstinate, inflexible and passive, waiting to be told what to do?

"We have reached the end of the 20th century and do not know what satisfies people or makes them happy! It can not be television or the football stadium. Theologians, sociologists and psychologists, philosophers, businessmen and trades unionists should consider how man can attain a sense of satisfaction in his work under the conditions of modern industrial society...

Once again, the answer lies in the variety of structural design possibilities

It is a question of finding a sensible demarcation between work and leisure. If there is more leisure time than working time, then in the case of a normal human being this disturbs the emotional balance. Work is then no longer a positive experience. There must be balanced working time in order to place demands on the human, so that he can perform in accordance with his talents, his training and his inclinations. We all know that we are only able to really enjoy our leisure time after work. It is a matter of the interplay between the two."   [F.W. Christians 1992]

Life is a combination of work and leisure

Let us recall how the role of the human in economic life was seen by the classic scholar of economic theory. Two hundred years ago, prior to the first industrial revolution, Adam Smith, whom we have already met in Chapter 2, painted the following picture of man in a market economy:

> "It is not from the benevolence of the butcher, the brewer, or the baker, that we expect our dinner, but from their regard to their own interest. We address ourselves, not to their humanity but to their self-love, and never talk to them of our own necessities but of their advantages." [Smith 1776]

The notion of man as a selfish creature acting in his own interests is over 200 years old

This 'homo oeconomicus' is therefore characterized by individualistic, even egoistical behavior: he thinks independently and acts rationally by striving for the greatest personal advantage. This principle is of course not always practiced in its extreme form and is present to a different degree in each individual, since, as we know, not all human actions are subject to the same rationality. But as a model, this observation comes close to a true image of man and can with some modification form the basis for our vision of humans within a fractal. Appeals to the intellect are therefore less effective than the opportunity to fulfil selfish desires under given conditions and constraints.

Homo oeconomicus is only a model, but this is close enough to reality to be used in our structural approach

In this model we also assume that as a rule each employee has a neutral relationship to his colleagues, i.e. that motives such as envy, spite, sympathy or benevolence are of secondary importance. Furthermore, we assume that an individual's behavior within the company will be exactly the same if structures other than the present ones exist, provided that the company's intrusion is limited to specifying clear objectives and providing the necessary resources and an efficient infrastructure (e.g. for information and communication). In such a system an

Each employee must sense his own usefulness, which is dependent on his performance. He must understand and accept the system in which he works

employee is aware of the usefulness of his own contribution. Management therefore delegates power and competences and the employee receives corresponding freedom of action but by necessity also assumes more of the responsibility and risk.

The Fractal Factory will soon become reality. This means that we do not need 'special people' to run it. We take what we have got, whether it is homo oeconomicus or simply the homo sapiens of our civilization. All we have to do is to give him the opportunities he needs to develop his enormous skills and to prevent him from indulging in his weaknesses. Of course, it is clear to us that these sublime requirements conceal a tremendous amount of effort - which we should not shrink from.

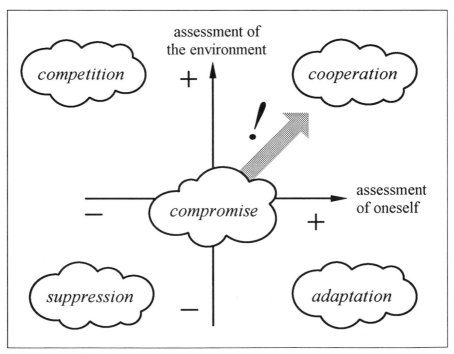

Fig. 70: The individual and his environment - today and tomorrow

The vision of the Fractal Factory contradicts the present situation in many ways: in management there are often opinions and practices to be found which exploit the needs of others for selfish purposes and which reward loyalty more than efficiency. Existing powers are used to the full to prevent the formation of independently viable structures. Such structures can only be formed if executive management exercises a high degree of self-control and subordinates personal goals to the corporate organization. Executives must not forget: to lead is to serve.

Management must sacrifice power and responsibility and develop its own self-image: to lead is to serve

"And 'tis a joy indeed how he inspires
And strengthens and revitalizes all around,
How every force asserts itself, how each gift
Becomes clearer when he is nigh!
From each man he draws forth the power
That is his very own, and nurtures it,
Lets each man remain what he is,
Watching only that he is ever so
In the right place; thus he knows how to
Make the strengths of all men unto his own."

Max Piccolomini on Wallenstein
Friedrich Schiller, 1797

The following example from working life may serve to show how far away we still are from Schiller's ideal of leadership:

"Mr. P., would you please come to the board room right away." This may seem quite innocuous, but on closer inspection it reveals great chasms behind the facade of many a company.

The case in question: We were asked by a medium-sized company to solve a technical problem. That it was in fact an organizational problem is another matter. The point here is the way an outsider experiences the corporate culture of a successful German company.

A corporate culture with a future: do not look for the guilty party. The productivity of German companies could be increased by 20 % by removing friction

After analyzing the existing situation we were in a position to clearly describe the roots of the problems and to illustrate possible solutions. This had the undesired effect of instigating a kind of trial of those in the line of responsibility. Instead of looking forward resolutely, the discussion was marked by such questions as: "is that true?" and "why is that still going on?" Thus the responsibility was implicitly passed on to those who had the day-to-day task of making the best out of the given situation.

During the course of the project we had the opportunity to speak to many members of staff and to see things from their point of view. The management had no confidence in the workforce and was looking for ways to restore full power to the spluttering engine through automation and by restricting the employees' freedom of action.

If we want to release the full potential of the workforce, we must obey the motto: do not be your own trouble spot

One production worker reported that he had been calling attention to deficiencies for a long time. And in most cases they could have been rectified easily. But since no response had been forthcoming he had lost interest in making this kind of effort on behalf of the company. This employee made quite clear that he no longer cared whether such problems were solved or not. After all, it was not his responsibility. Neither an organized system for making improvement suggestions nor a relevant incentive system associated with it existed.

Another skilled worker reported that 'campaigns' were initiated at regular intervals, e.g. cost-reduction exercises. But because no clear concept existed, these measures contradicted one another. No clear path was in evidence. The staff inevitably came to have doubts about the management's methods. The best way to cope with this kind of situation is to just carry out instructions and to stop thinking about it. On the notice board a 'barrack-room inspection' is announced: a factory visitation is to take place on the following Friday to check that everything is neat and tidy...

Acceptance can only be obtained if the persons concerned are involved in the preparation of measures

And so the cycle is closed: the relationship between management and staff is dominated by indifference and mistrust. The mechanisms in place serve to cement this condition. Everyone concerned is able to justify his decisions and actions logically. But this is not the way out of such an entrenched situation.

As we have already observed, the company is operating successfully in the marketplace. So the persons responsible are not plagued by self-doubts. All decisions and measures taken in the past had been accompanied by economic success in terms of growth rates and therefore seemed to be 'right'. The fact that this was rather due to favorable external conditions had gone overlooked. In this example the vicious circle can only be broken by a change in management behavior.

Success in the marketplace masks management errors; this makes the impact of hard times much greater

In realizing the Fractal Factory we will be breaking open ossified structures. We can expect tough resistance which we shall have to overcome by creating broad acceptance of our proposals.

*Clinging to posi-
tions of power is
an obstacle to the
necessary process
of adaptation, and
makes its eventual
implementation
much harder to
bear*

The level of most resistance in our factories is to be found amongst the lower echelons of management. As a rule this means the foreman. This is due to his traditional position in the company. He is the undisputed authority within the scope of his responsibility and in many cases maintaining this position of power becomes a personal goal which is pursued with all means available. But a transfer of responsibility to operators involves a transfer of competences. This can result in what could mildly be called 'friction'. Here, too, it is easy to find a suitable case study on the subject:

A young design engineer, full of enthusiasm, joined the process development division of a reputable and successful company. He was given freedom to develop new production processes independently and creatively. Skilled workers were assigned to him to enable the machines to be tested. Soon he was complaining about the lack of motivation amongst these workers. Tasks entrusted to them were not being performed satisfactorily. At the smallest technical difficulty the maintenance men were called for, which wasted a great deal of time. There was no sign of independent initiative; it was more like a 'work to rule'. This first experience of practice came as a shock to the young engineer, all the more so since he had become accustomed to a forthright and determined, goal-oriented way of working during his training.

In an agonizing process of learning he was forced to admit that he was powerless against an apparatus in which each member knew his exact place and had precise competences and exploited this situation to its limits. And

*We need our
energies to face
global economic
competition, not
for internal strife.
Companies and
employees' coun-
cils who realize
this make jobs
secure and ensure
survival of the
company*

whereas the union had played a strangely passive role in the first example we looked at, in the second one it dominated the whole network of relationships throughout a large concern.

So does the Fractal Factory fail because of the human element? No. This optimism is based on history: whole branches of industry have all too often undergone radical change and humans have always actively pursued this process even if sometimes only after a considerable delay. This process is in fact already under way, since authoritative structures have long been losing ground in our society.

The Fractal Factory does not fail because of humans

In addition, the particular skills which humans have embody precisely the potentials which should be encouraged and exploited by a Fractal Factory. The prerequirements are satisfied.

"I know that every normal, feeling person wants to show what he can do. That is why he must be permitted to show it. At least half of the things which are attributed to oneself have, in fact, been achieved by hard-working assistants, who, however, first had to be found and entrusted with the respective tasks."   [F.W. Christians 1992]

At the middle levels of the hierarchy people can often be found who know how to delegate, motivate and communicate. But this type of successful team manager often suffers from the disadvantage of not setting high enough standards and allowing too many exceptions. After all, he has to master the difficult task of being a superior and a subordinate at the same time. The human potential of these managers makes them indispensible even when the number of

In the Fractal Factory the demand for leadership and staff with leadership qualifications is greater, not lesser

hierarchical levels is reduced. And what is more, their wealth of knowledge and experience is needed in large measure.

Many more members of staff with leadership qualifications are needed now than ever before, since each group must be led. For this, the ability to work together with colleagues and specialists from various areas such as marketing and distribution or research and development is a particular advantage. The ability to cooperate with colleagues who have different goals, interests and ambitions and to whom they can not give orders to as in a hierarchical 'pecking order', requires new qualifications.

New leadership qualifications are required: management by persuasion, not by decree

On top of this, they must have the ability to break down the executive management's targets into sub-goals and tasks and to ensure their fulfilment. Consistent decentralization results in independently responsible and result-conscious employees. During this transition to more complex, more strategically market-oriented tasks they need the support of senior management.

The "mature worker" is still out of place in collective bargaining

The solution which we envisage in the Fractal Factory touches base at this point. All characteristics referred to at the beginning of this chapter are designed to guarantee support for as many solutions as possible taking into account the interaction of sociopolitical factors.

Both sides of industry must think in terms of the future and must move with the times, otherwise they will become obsolete

Such considerations effect both sides of industry. Today's wage agreements are based on the assumption of a largely united workforce whose interests can be reduced to the idea of 'more money for less work'. And here, too, it should be a matter of 'more freedom and less exercise of power'. But this means that for both management and unions it will not become easier,

History teaches us of the fall of rigid, unimaginative structures whose only thought is to hang on to power

but more difficult and more demanding to run, influence and design such factories.

Decades ago, sociological concepts existed which point us in the direction we are heading in today. In 1944 the Nobel Prize winner, Friedrich August von Hajek (1899-1992) published his thoughts on a social philosophy in the center of which was the idea of 'spontaneous order' [Bouillon 1991]. The thesis is that an order which develops spontaneously is always superior to a planned order. The roots of this lie in the limitations of human insight and articulation. We can only plan to a limited degree of complexity. So a spontaneous order which is determined by independently acting individuals and which does not follow a plan, can be much more efficient in spite of its complexity. The classic example of this is the market economy, which brings about a high degree of prosperity and leads to the fulfilment of many needs by virtue of free human activity - which is not the case in planned and centralized orders, as the last seventy years have made blatantly clear. Spontaneous systems are subject to a constant process of evolution towards an ideal adaptation under the influence of changing events and circumstances as we are familiar with in the case of living organisms. Previously we assumed this adaptation to be the task of the employer, the board of directors or the president, but the more complex and turbulent the environment becomes, the more management is overburdened or simply can not afford to expend so much capacity on this task. The result is then the necessity for such directives as, "in order to reduce costs, staff levels must be cut by ten percent across the board." Or only such investments are sanctioned which will be paid

An order which develops spontaneously, such as a market economy, is always better than a planned order

Systems planning fails in the face of unquantifiable complexity. Factories are complex systems which are permanently subjected to outside influences - from customers

Senior management is stretched to the limit; this results in rigid, generalized measures

off in a period of less than a year. In other words, management often capitulates under the complexity of the situation and resorts to rigid regulations. In larger corporations in particular, this can lead to the company being 'regulated to death' as far as the exploitation of staff potential is concerned.

We must not lose sight of the fact that dealing with people means dealing with individuals, who will stubbornly resist any kind of 'formalization'. Indeed, the expression itself sounds shocking in this context, and a good thing, too! Whereas statistical approaches fail under these conditions, the management of a Fractal Factory rejoices at them; homogeneity and one-dimensionality are anathema to them.

A spontaneous order is not welcomed by all

In a factory we usually find two types of employee: some are open-minded, willing and able to apply knowledge and experience above and beyond their own domain in order to achieve global, holistic objectives, others reject more complex demands and prefer only to carry out prescribed and clearly defined tasks. When we speak to the former, we are usually surprised and astonished to learn the kind of activities and hobbies they pursue in their free time, involving a high degree of creativity and intensity. And once again we see how critical it is to be able to remould these potentials into useful factors of industrial production.

Increased automation enhances the importance of the workers for the company. A few years ago the opposite was feared, or even aimed for

With the majority of existing manufacturing systems, individuals have no opportunity at all to influence the design of their working environment. For a time the march of automation even gave rise to the idea of eliminating humans as a 'disruptive factor' in manufacturing systems. The ideal preconditions for this seemed to be supplied by the dazzling pace of developments in microelectronics. Computer controlled, flexible manufacturing systems opened up the possibility of bridging the chasm between productivity and flexibility. Not too long ago informed circles were anticipating a fall in the level of qualifications required by the workforce because only supervisory functions and residual operations such as in- and outfeeding of the production line would have to be performed manually. The Fractal Factory on the other hand requires human design intervention at all levels. This does not only apply to purely physical operations but also to general tasks such as administration and organization.

This thesis was impressively substantiated by H. Hammer at the Colloquium on Manufacturing Technology in 1991. The shop floor activities of thirteen flexible manufacturing systems were examined in an empirical survey. All machinery came from the same manufacturer, so, unlike in many surveys, the subject of the study could be considered to be homogeneous. The level of efficiency of the systems ranged from 65 to 95 percent.

The wide range of stoppage causes is reflected equally in both technical and organizational areas:

- technical failure rate: 1 - 19 percent
- organizational failure rate: 1 - 24 percent.

This, however, does not give us any indication of the real reasons for the wide disparity in efficiency levels. The survey was able to show that

- type of production (flow, batch or job production)

Qualification and motivation - the latter mainly through acceptance and participation in benefits - are vital for productivity and flexibility

- quantity of different workpieces
- production cycle
- workpiece complexity (expressed by the number of tools)
- job change frequency
- shift system and
- size of workforce

had no significant influence on shop-floor behavior. On the other hand the factors of

- staff qualification and
- workforce motivation

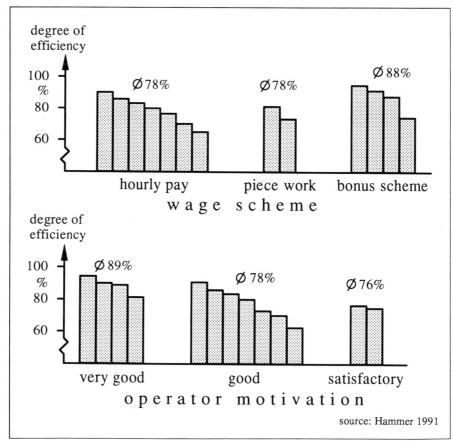

Fig. 71: Factors affecting efficiency in flexible manufacturing systems

had a considerable influence. It is a fact that 95 percent of breakdowns can be dealt with without calling in the manufacturers. The vast majority of failures are due to minor defects which can be rectified quickly if the relevant knowledge is available. The companies running these systems have learned this from many years of experience and so the level of training amongst their machine operators is consistently very high.

95 % of faults occurring can be rectified immediately

There are differences, though, when it comes to the system of payments: both hourly pay and piecework result in about ten percent less efficiency than an incentive scheme. Similar differences in efficiency levels are attributable to the degree of satisfaction of the machine operators with the system conception.

It is worthwhile to inform and train the workforce

General Motors' Saturn Project was one of the most ambitious projects for a future-oriented manufacturing plant in recent years. The concept is based on a high degree of automation, extensive networking of computer-controlled manufacturing facilities and a concentration of the whole value creation chain (from casting to despatch) in a single location. In its original form, direct labor costs were to be reduced by more than half through automation. Then, however, tight financial constraints and technical difficulties led to a shift of objectives towards a combination of conventional and automated production stages.

Performance and productivity related pay structures will become more common at all levels

Technology can not replace man, but it can help him and multiply his output

"When a factory possesses state-of-the-art manufacturing facilities requiring more attention to be paid to the machines than to the products, then the investment is in vain," is now the verdict of Jim Lewandowski, Vice President of Saturn People Systems. Success can not be forced through technology. Technology can only be a "means to aid people in the manufacture of high-quality goods." Here, as in many other automobile factories, emphasis is now being placed on group-work with a considerable degree of autonomy.

In matters of production, group technology shows us the way to the Fractal Factory

It becomes clear from this case-study that focussing on technology-dominated structures does not in itself offer a guarantee of success. The human dominance in the manufacturing process postulated in the Fractal Factory can also be found in other recent concepts. E. Ulich describes the restructuring of the PCB assembly unit at Landis&Gyr AG:

"The daily work program is usually specified by the foreman or supervisor and the workers coordinate it according to internal consensus amongst themselves, which however is made more difficult by linguistic and cultural differences (seven nationalities).

The constraint of having to process the plated PCB's within three hours means that daily production planning must take place within the group and that it is necessary for as many group members as possible to be able to work at any of the various stations. So employees are required to change workplaces relatively frequently, which is welcomed by the majority of staff.

The organizational and physical proximity of all concerned proves to be beneficial

The organizational and physical proximity of the technical department leads to frequent contact between production workers and technicians. If technical problems have to be solved or the assembly machines reprogrammed, the operators are directly present and can follow the problem-solving process.

This provides many opportunities for learning. An indication of how conducive this scheme is to learning is a discussion microscope to be found in the department. This instrument enables two people to simultaneously observe and discuss a specimen and the staff are very keen to take advantage of it."

[Ulich 1989]

But experiences with group technology are ambivalent, as a further case study from the automotive industry shows:

"An important problem is that it is not possible to work ahead. If a vehicle with a lower labor content than the lamp cycle is being worked on and the vehicle is left to stand until the light goes on, then it can easily happen, that someone else, the foreman for example, may come along and insist on the car being finished. This is a constant source of trouble, although there are now certain tricks. For example, a worker may, instead of releasing the car he has finished working on, proceed to the second car, which is already waiting in line, and work ahead on this one. Then he releases the first car and has all the time for the second car available as a time buffer for himself. But the problem is that everything is now exposed; everybody can see if someone is not at his own workplace. At a conveyor belt nobody used to care if another person worked ahead; the foreman knew what was going on when he saw someone having a cigarette somewhere, but at the same time he knew that they had obviously worked ahead and that everything was running smoothly."

[Jürgens 1989]

As far as the organization of group work is concerned, we are still in the process of learning

Negative experience must not deter us. It is often the result of incorrect design

The rate of absenteeism can be influenced by developing a sense of responsibility

The Scandavian countries were in the vanguard of GT concepts. Sweden in particular led the field in the seventies. But it must not be forgotten that the shortage of skilled staff prevailing there and the rate of absenteeism meant that jobs had to be made as attractive as possible very early on. Saab's futuristic engine plant in Malmö attracted a great deal of attention, but it had to be closed about a year after opening. Group concepts have so far failed because productivity and creativity fall off after a certain time (fig. 72). In dynamical systems, on the other hand, it is possible to maintain a high level of performance over a long period of time.

So let us summarize: it is not a contradiction for humans to work in a highly automated environment. On the contrary, in many cases it is this that makes manufacturing an economic

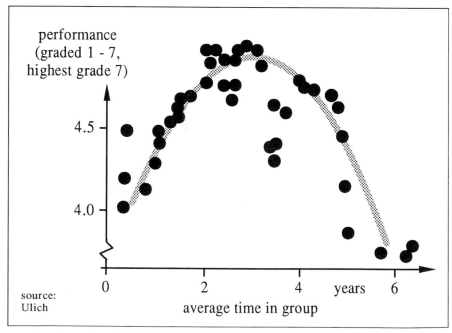

Fig. 72: Performance curve of project groups

proposition. Workers must be released from their role as mere operators in the process. They must be turned into plant leaders requiring the appropriate training and qualifications. All the same, a manufacturing system based entirely on humans soon reaches its limitations. Nor will cost-effective manufacturing be possible in the future without using processes that involve a high degree of specialization and certain technical constraints.

Technical constraints can not be avoided in future. They affect process design

These latter examples clearly show that it is not enough to simply dress up old ideas in new clothes, which in our case means simply labelling any number of organized group concepts unquestioningly as 'fractal'. Rather, we must try harder to incorporate the personal human goals within a wider structure, or more precisely within a framework of objectives, in such a way that individual and global goals harmonize. Goal conformity is the key to the maximum exploitation of human resources in the Fractal Factory. This strategic resource can be more easily tapped through the principle of self-similarity, which also ensures that the needs of the staff are not bypassed.

Personal goals must be incorporated into a suitable design framework

When we consider the role of humans in a fractal we can not avoid discussing corporate culture or, to use another term, company ethics. There is a drastically growing need for communication here: information about goals, values, ideas and concrete actions must be continually exchanged between the fractals, from above and from below, but primarily in external dealings. Communication is a basic function of a vital system. Such considerations must begin where the main potentials reside: in man. And he can only navigate successfully in a complex environment if he is in a position to correctly

One disadvantage of the market economy is the dependence of the worker on the quality of management; the workforce must therefore become more involved

estimate both his own position and the positions of other units and the directions in which they are moving [Kühnle 1993].

An example shall serve to illustrate the necessity for this approach:

Any participation in decision making or in the success of a company must involve more responsibility and higher risk

In the sales department of a major German concern there was, to put it mildly, uncertainty about the firm's objectives. The result was a deep mistrust of all the management's actions and a large number of employees withdrew from any active participation in corporate processes into a small sphere of activity which they could handle well. The identification of the workforce with the company and its products, which had been a traditional strength of the company for many decades, had practically vanished. As the reason for this, those concerned unanimously

---

Communication-oriented structures are needed to maintain the force of innovation within an organization!

from organization ad rem	to organization ad personam
from functional specialization	to interdisciplinary generalization
from the search for synergy	to competition between units
from an emphasis on hierarchy and status	to horizontal communication and cooperation
from inherent centralism	to decentralized, shallow structure
from external organization	to self-organization

source: Höhler 1992

Fig. 73: Strategic communication within a company

cited the complete lack of any communicative confidence-building measures on the part of senior management. The need for organizational intervention was not revealed. Teams of consultants were operating in the company without receiving any informational support, which middle management resisted by all means possible, in particular by sealing itself off completely. Significant performance shortcomings in almost all areas were becoming a growing problem. Statements such as 'the only thing I can expect from this place, is that they pay me my money' were not infrequent.

A shortcoming: lack of confidence-building communication

In spite of all expectations with regard to improvements for humans in the Fractal Factory, we must not lose sight either of technology nor the other critical success factors of a company. Even cost reduction programs, for ever tainted with the image of being inhuman measures, can bring positive results. We have already referred to the survey carried out by Blaxill and Hout, in which they report on an American firm which scrapped its plans for drastic cost-reduction measures after a visit to the factory of one of their Japanese affiliates:

Cost reduction programs must question structures

This comparable company was far more decentralized and had a flatter, more cellular organizational structure. The equipment uptime was high, rework stations did not exist and the WIP inventory was low. The overhead for a similar volume of production was not even half as high as that of the American company. A cross-functional working group was formed with the task of redefining the company's job functions and processes. Individual overhead employees

Multifunctional working groups show us the way to new structures

*Indirect cost
personnel must
be evaluated
according to their
contribution to
value-creation*

were assessed according to the contribution they made and then three categories of indirect staff were established:

- *core management* (general manager, facilities-maintenance staff and production control engineers)
- *process improvers* (R & D engineers, process and materials engineers and purchasing managers)
- *problem fixers* (inspectors, expediters, automation experts and troubleshooters).

*Integration and
cooperation are
secrets of success*

But this alone is still not enough. A multi-functional working group must be installed around the product and its production and must think in terms of systems in order to develop subtle ways of dealing with the interplay between people, machines, processes and materials. Each of these units is self-correcting and refuses to accept inadequate inputs. The secret of success is therefore integration and cooperation.   [Blaxill 1991]

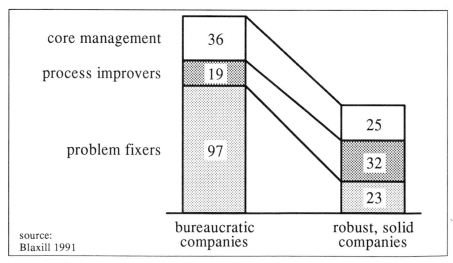

core management — 36
process improvers — 19
problem fixers — 97

25
32
23

bureaucratic companies   robust, solid companies

source:
Blaxill 1991

Fig. 74: Overhead staff comparison of two competitors

The Fractal Factory will place greater demands on the qualifications of the workforce. But this is in line with tendencies already under way: training programs in the metal industry have already been adapted to the new situation and their content is now designed to meet these new, extended demands. Available training opportunities can now be called up via databases to which even small and medium-sized companies have access, although awareness of this facility is not yet very widespread and it is hardly taken advantage of, in spite of the fact that all chambers of commerce and industry are connected to the vocational training information service. The database operated by the Association of German Chambers of Industry and Commerce and the German Association of Chambers of Handicraft Trades currently contains about 10,000 vocational training opportunities.

Vocational training must have a strong practical content

There is no doubt that generalists will feel more at home in the new environment than specialists. But the latter will by no means become redundant. Otherwise there is the danger of losing important know-how within a few years, both in manufacturing and also in product development. As far as the introverted, ingenious tinkerer is concerned, a suitable fractal will be built in which he can fully develop his creativity. This would correspond to a staff function. The tendency will be for specialists to disappear from the operative level and to make themselves available in the form of service fractals.

Specialists whose capacities are not fully taken advantage of must be transferred to a service fractal

Performance assessment and evaluation

Even though there are conflicting statements on the subject of performance assessment, the

Financial incentives will remain important in future

most effective motivational force is still based on financial incentives and there is no indication that anything is likely to change here. From the company's point of view it is therefore essential to choose the correct standard by which to measure performance. In the case of a fractal, this is goal attainment.

In a fractal, all members contribute to goal attainment. The group's performance is therefore evaluated as a whole

In the wider sense, systems for measuring and evaluating performance may be counted among the control instruments. The most important tie between fractals is the self-similar goal system. The performance of a fractal is measured by the degree of goal attainment. This value is permanently available via the information system and therefore performance assessment and evaluation always refer to the whole fractal and not to individual machines or persons.

Group bonuses are becoming more popular

This takes advantage of the insight that many of the performance assessment criteria used today are unsatisfactory. High machine availability, for example, can be obtained at the expense of excessive operation and maintenance. But all these factors are defined in the goal system and weighted against each other. The degree of goal

specialist	generalist
- provides know-how	- coordinates
- uses experience, intuition	- uses communication nodes
- provides continuity	- provides new ideas
- achieves goals	- sets goals

Fig. 75: Complementary skills of specialists and generalists

attainment is therefore a very meaningful standard which should also be used in the calculation of incentive bonuses. In practice, group-related performance evaluation is already being successfully implemented - for three reasons:

- Individual performance assessment usually involves a great deal of administration and control work.
- The performance of automated manufacturing systems is not usually attributable to a single person.
- The group is responsible for determining its own performance curve. The performance potential of group members is fully exploited.

This system is nowadays strongly favored by management because it removes many previous causes of conflict. All these advantages taken together justify assigning members of staff to higher wage groups. In many places the strong-

Pay schemes can remove possible causes of conflict

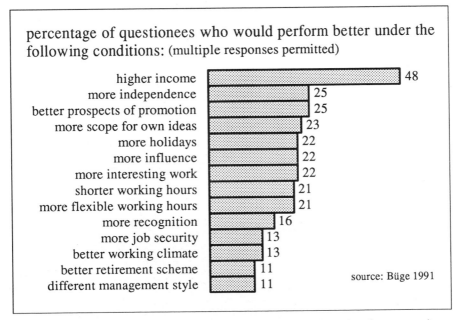

percentage of questionees who would perform better under the following conditions: (multiple responses permitted)

higher income	48
more independence	25
better prospects of promotion	25
more scope for own ideas	23
more holidays	22
more influence	22
more interesting work	22
shorter working hours	21
more flexible working hours	21
more recognition	16
more job security	13
better working climate	13
better retirement scheme	11
different management style	11

source: Büge 1991

Fig. 76: Motivation factors for the workforce (result of a survey)

est argument for this is provided by simply enquiring after the real cost of determining piece rates.

Recently there has been movement in the previously rigid wage structures, due in large measure to the fact that it is often impossible to influence the production cycle in highly automated manufacturing processes and so this can not be used as a basis for pay calculation. In such cases the availability of the manufacturing system is much more important. Performance evaluation on the basis of this parameter leads, as we have seen, to tangible improvements.

Hourly pay has not passed the test

Fig. 77 shows that companies have been responding to this over the last ten years. The temporary increase in hourly-paid work may be seen as an (unsatisfactory) transitional stage.

It is fundamentally possible to develop a pay structure according to the characteristics 'performance-related' and 'demand-related'.

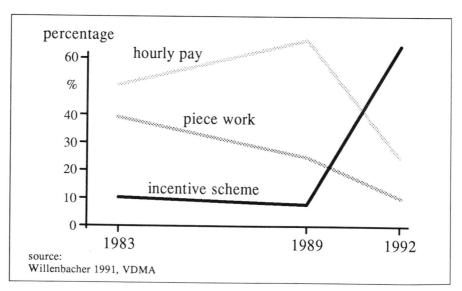

Fig. 77: The development of pay schemes

Such a system, which as a rule is company-specific, can include one or more of these fields. In many quarters the strong differentiation between pay structures for blue and white collar workers is increasingly coming to be regarded with disfavor. At Siemens, for example, the basic salary of office staff is automatically incremented (based on the effect of an assumed learning curve), whereas pay for skilled staff is linked to the job specification level. As a result, financial improvements come much more quickly and easily to office staff (fig. 78).

The distinction between white and blue collar workers is becoming harder to justify. It results in a dequalification at production level

This distinction becomes especially problematic as the borderline between blue and white collar workers becomes even vaguer, which is currently a marked trend as a result of organizational changes. In the light of this a unified pay structure for both categories of employees was developed about 20 years ago at Siemens, but was never implemented in Germany due to difficulties with collective bargaining legislation. A subsidiary in Switzerland, on the other hand,

It is time for a change in pay structures

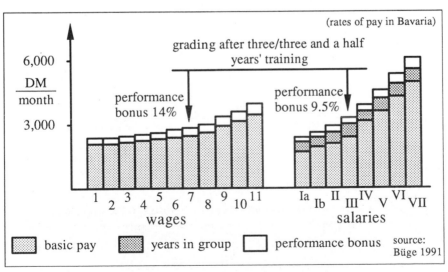

Fig. 78: Wages and salaries at Siemens

experienced positive results from its introduction. All the signs indicate that the time is now ripe for a fundamental change of this nature.

In a fractal, pay includes a heterogeneous component

Because of the heterogeneous structure of qualifications within a fractal, it is necessary to solve the goal-conflict between specification and performance related pay components. The following example demonstrates that this is possible:

> "The company ... manufactures machines and equipment in job and batch production. Part of the production was converted to semi-autonomous groups. Because of the low batch quantity and the consequently high level of scheduling and control work, the influence of indirect areas ... on performance was very high. In addition to the duties performed by production workers, those of staff in indirect areas also had to be integrated into the organizational unit.

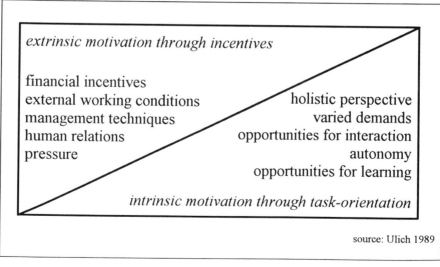

extrinsic motivation through incentives

financial incentives
external working conditions
management techniques
human relations
pressure

holistic perspective
varied demands
opportunities for interaction
autonomy
opportunities for learning

intrinsic motivation through task-orientation

source: Ulich 1989

Fig. 79: Opening up motivational potentials

In order to enable the employees to participate in the success of their work, consideration was given to a performance-related pay
scheme... From the point of view of the factory, peformance-related pay makes good
sense as a means of providing extrinsic motivation in addition to the intrinsic motivation
offered by the partially autonomous group.

*The workforce
must participate in
the success of their
work - but in a
flexible way; the
bonus must be able
to fall when times
are hard*

The productivity bonus can be distributed
according to four different procedures:

- in equal and absolute sums of money distributed among all staff (per capita)
- as equal percentages of the basic salary
- in accordance with assessment criteria,
  e.g. evaluation of conduct and performance
- through a combination of these procedures.

The company opted for the latter form of distribution of the productivity bonus. The bonus
for the semi-autonomous group was divided
into two equal halves. One half was paid in
equal and absolute cash value to all staff and
the other half in equal percentages of basic
pay.

This method succeeds in keeping down ... the
range of bonuses in order not to have a detrimental effect on the motivation of lower
wage-groups ... and on the other hand main-
tains differentials so that the bonus ... remains
'tangible' for technical staff. The distribution
of one half according to a head count
acknowledges the fact that a chain is only as
strong as its weakest link."   [Eyer 1991]

*We need new pilot
projects to help us
find new solutions*

This and further examples show that we are
already on the right track. However, there
remains a tendency to use available criteria -
through operational data collection, for example

- as a basis for evaluation, and often this is not ideal. Against this background the concept of goal-oriented fractals seems very promising.

Working hours

The working week has been a controversial subject for a number of years now. This problem will hardly go away in the age of the Fractal Factory. New requirements emerge with regard to the coordination of change-over times.

Efficient communications systems and simultaneous decentralization contribute to the flexibility of working hours

In the past everything was much easier: the works siren gave the signal for the factory to close and all workers and staff poured out of the factory gates and went home. At the same time the late shift began. The days in which whole towns pulsed to the formula $3 \times 8 = 24$ are for the most part long gone, not least of all because of the considerable expansion that has taken place in the service sector. We shall not even mention traffic problems in this connection, even though they are an important marginal consideration in attempts to break-up the old system.

There are now many hundreds of models

Flexible working hours were introduced in administrative areas as early as the seventies. For a long time it was considered unthinkable to transfer such models to the industrial sector, especially in a system based on the division of labor. But by 1985 at the latest - with the introduction of agreements on the reduction of working hours - the matter had become acute. Now there are several hundred plans which are supposed to bring collective wage agreements and company interests into harmony. No doubt we are in the midst of a transitional phase and many of these schemes are only of a temporary nature. When the 35-hour week is introduced in the metal industry in 1995 there will be still more new models.

It is not our purpose here to take sides for or against this trend. Rather, we wish to recognize and exploit the opportunities and possibilities offered by new working hours regulations. Of course there will be increased flexibility and individualization, but in spite of all regulations it remains a fact that any decision in favor of a particular job, profession, function or activity determines, or at least has a considerable influence on, the hours to be worked in a week or year.

Collective pay agreements can only provide a framework. Today there are already many examples of individual arrangements

From the wide range of such aspects let us consider the subject of flexitime [Wagener 1991]. At the firm of Stihl in Waiblingen, a leading manufacturer of power saws, two shifts are operated for equipment manufacture in order to better exploit the CNC machines. Significantly, the hours scheme was worked out largely by the employees concerned.

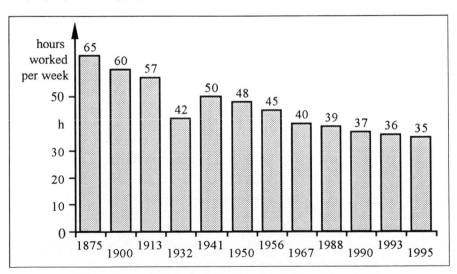

Fig. 80: Development of the working week in Germany

The employees concerned develop their own system of working hours in the interests of maximum machine exploitation

For the hand-over from early to late shift there is a window of three and a half hours available. It is therefore absolutely essential that effective coordination between the individual members of staff takes place, and in practice this works quite well. Shifts overlap by 15 minutes in order to facilitate hand-over. This provides enough latitude for immediate agreements to be reached on personal matters (e.g. time for official visits). It goes without saying that the work is divided up in a largely autonomous process, since there are considerable blocks of flexible time for structuring both at the beginning and at the end of the working day (fig. 81).

Computer-aided systems make time keeping and wage calculation more economical

The operational work required to administer this shift system is minimal since it is limited to time keeping and calculation. It is all the more amazing how well the system works because the critical coordination activity takes place

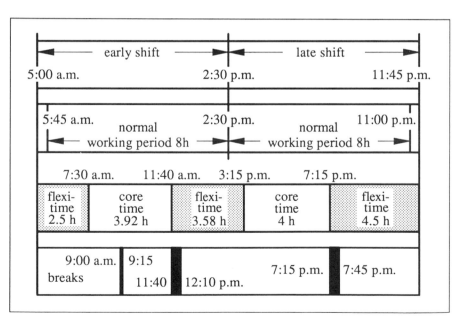

Fig. 81: Flexitime scheme at Stihl

between members of staff who only meet for a few minutes each day and yet function as a practiced team.

In the next few years the spread of non-working shifts will bring about new coordination problems. As far as the working hours of a given individual are concerned, the exception will almost become the rule. It will remain absolutely essential to exploit machine capacity to the full by offering attractive working conditions, not least through attractive working hours. It is obvious that these unpredictable conditions are best dealt with by self-organized systems, in other words in a Fractal Factory, supported by an efficient information and communications system.

The Fractal Factory also permits self-organization and manageability in matters of working hours

The way to the Fractal Factory - an exemplary case-study

It is of course easiest to talk about a difficult situation in a factory after it has been overcome. The firm of Sulzer-Weise, a manufacturer of pumps located in Bruchsal in Baden, today finds itself in this enviable position. With its payroll of 500 industrial staff and a wide range of products it can be considered a typical medium-sized company.

A crisis is often needed to provide the stimulus for new ideas

Three years ago the company was in the throes of a deep crisis. The continued existence of the manufacturing site was seriously endangered and a reduction in the workforce seemed inevitable. The causes were not sought in external influences but within the company itself. The symptoms were obvious to the management team: WIP inventories were piling up in the production department and delivery delays on

customer orders were taking on grotesque proportions. This in turn resulted in a weakened
market position.

The climate in the company was extremely cold
at the time. At that point in time the management could not envisage the possibility of constructive collaboration with the unions in the
conceivable future and the result was a correspondingly high staff turnover.

*Humans had been
neglected as a
production factor
for too long*

This case must not be considered extreme. In
another aspect, too, the company can be
thought of as exemplary: in the eighties a range
of rationalization projects had been embarked
upon, from computer-aided design and production planning to flexible manufacturing. Once
again we see an attempt to overcome a company's problems entirely through the enforced
introduction of new technology. Only with
hindsight does it become clear how deep-seated
the mechanistic and deterministic view of the
world was in the factory at that time.

*We must invest in
the workforce*

The decision makers were only too aware that
things could not go on as they were. Starting
from the knowledge that many years of experience had given the company good control of
both technology and structures whereas humans
had been neglected as a production factor for
just as long, a concept was developed which
bore fruit in a very short time.

Since staff management was being conducted
entirely according to familiar and obviously no
longer viable methods, a 'trainer' was engaged
who had witnessed the entire process of transformation. In two-day workshops awareness of
the actual problems of the company was
enhanced. So far, sixty percent of the workforce

have taken part in such meetings, and the desire to continue is clearly coming 'from below'.

According to those concerned, the situation in the company has now drastically changed. People have "found a different way of getting along with each other." All departmentalized thinking has vanished; it is as if the workforce had been renewed. The most important thing is agreement on the goals before such a measure is embarked upon. In the event of subsequent contradictions and conflicts it is normally enough to refer to this agreement in order to objectify, and usually to solve, the problem. This applies especially to lower and middle management, whereby it should be remarked that the company had previously believed that it would be necessary to dispense with the services of a number of these employees.

People learn to get on better

The costs for human resources development schemes are not insignificant. Initially, they amounted to 20 percent of the investment budget, but since then they have been falling steadily. The mediator referred to is in the company almost full-time, which shows how important his activity is. Furthermore, he participates equally in discussions with the management and with the workers' representatives, which underlines his competence and ability to integrate.

20 % of the investment budget was spent on human resources projects

In this way the path was smoothed for structures and procedures in which the characteristics of the Fractal Factory are to be found. From planning work on a flexible manufacturing system - which, for reasons we have already discussed, was not realized - classes of workpieces could be identified which are similar from a production point of view: casings, laminas, shafts and small parts. For the produc-

It is not always possible to specify precise targets, nor is it necessary

tion of these parts fractals with a high degree of autonomy were formed to work in two shifts. These islands of seven to twenty-eight workers per shift each have a weekly program to complete. More specific planning is consciously dispensed with, or rather it is left up to the workers themselves. In view of the wide range of parts this is no mean task, since many criteria have to be considered, some of which are 'unclear', i.e. they can not be described in detail. But on the basis of experience so far, the principle has proved to be successful across the whole range.

We must overcome fear of change

Initially, piece work and time-related pay schemes were operated in parallel. A survey revealed (of course) that the efficiency level for piece work was equal to the prescribed 'sound barrier', in this case 135 percent. Hourly paid workers achieved between 40 and 100, on an average 70 percent. So contrary to many people's expectations, the hourly-paid workers were by far the 'most expensive'. In the fractals, a veritable 'performance explosion' was observed amongst this group; the comparative figure is now 120 percent. Lead times have fallen by 30 to 40 percent. There is no longer any stockpiling of work in progress; raw material is available on call from stock, as determined by the fractal concerned and not by a central administration!

The fear of change which had been particularly strong amongst the workforce who had previously been paid an hourly rate was very quickly overcome. Contrary to expectations, collaboration between workers of different age groups proved to be beneficial.

The workforce is now paid according to productivity, in the form of bonuses, divided as a matter of principle equally amongst the whole group, taking both shifts together. The group has an elected speaker who has a full work load and receives no financial reward. This prevents the position of foreman from being secretly re-established, an effect which can be observed in many other examples of group working. The large reserve of potential speakers is in itself amazing; the figure is over 50 percent. The fear which is occasionally expressed that the pay scheme in such a group must result in a harsh social climate, is not borne out here. The performance differentials which inevitably arise do not result in individuals being ostracized, which must be due at least in part to the attention paid to human factors.

Hierarchies are also dismantled in the pay structure

The group integrates poor performers

Meetings of all fractal employees take place at regular intervals, as a rule weekly, and notes of these meetings are taken as a matter of principle. They deal mainly with efficiency improvements, since these are in the natural interest of the employees.

Regular meetings complement constant, spontaneous communication

After all this has been said, one could obtain the impression that all the developments of recent years on the machine and computer side have been thrown over board. The opposite is the case. For one thing, state-of-the-art machines (DNC operation) are used, and for another the whole job process is controlled by a computer system specially adapted to the requirements of the factory. The company now has 380 terminals, which are actually in use. Each employee has access to job data. The widespread view that certain age groups would not accept these systems has proven to be untrue. Job control is carried out by only four members of staff, who

Automation and information penetration are constantly being promoted

Amazing: a simple system makes it possible to control complex processes

compile the respective weekly schedules for each fractal. For this, they only consider the main machines and therefore the critical capacities. For all other machines only a rough capacity estimate is made. The impressive aspect of the whole system is its simplicity. The company still has to overcome the problem of missing interfaces between software systems installed over the years: for technical drawings, NC-programs, production scheduling and order processing. But in this respect it is in the same position as many other companies.

In administrative divisions we are at the very beginning of the road to the Fractal Factory

It is proving considerably more difficult to establish fractal structures in administrative areas. Here, 'kingdoms' have to be dissolved which over the years and even decades have been turned into hereditary courts. Middle management has proved to be particularly 'resistant' and in the end the function of group manager was abolished altogether. In its place there are only the team leaders of the project groups, which are formed on a temporary basis. This results in interdisciplinary cooperation, for which office space is made available as the need arises. Work is currently under way to establish a corporate model in which each employee's self-image and that of the company are expressed to the customers.

We must force the conversion to the Fractal Factory

This example clearly shows the three characteristics of 'self-similarity', 'self-organization' and 'dynamics'. However, not all methods and aids of the Fractal Factory have been implemented in this instance. The transformation will never be complete. It is therefore not enough for interested companies to copy the structures described, particularly since many solutions would have to take on a different shape in another factory. Nor does the management of

Sulzer-Weise have any fear of losing its clear competitive edge as a result of these revelations. Each company will have to go its own way and this may lead to different goals via different paths. Transferring responsibility will certainly not make it easier to run an industrial corporation. It is precisely the extra attention which must be devoted to treating employees as human beings which will confront managerial staff with tasks for which their training has not prepared them and for which many are sure to lack the skills.

We must therefore disappoint those readers who expect to find an organizational chart of the Fractal Factory at this point, simply because it does not exist, and can not exist, in general terms. Experience gained through the introduction of CIM concepts into operational practice has provided us with an insight which should perhaps be obvious: just as with new processes, new forms of organization must undergo a period of incubation and can not be introduced from one day to the next. This will be no different in the case of the Fractal Factory.

Each company must go its own way; imitation is only possible in very general terms

The development process takes time; we must not rush in; this way we avoid mistakes

However, the stage seems to be set for this gradual development: isolated elements of the Fractal Factory can already be found in daily practice. Specific examples of this are the formation of business units, an orientation towards business processes, the introduction of manufacturing segmentation and cellular production structures, not to mention the trend towards group technology. A process of consolidation will once again demonstrate that even this does not contain the solution to all problems - as some executives continue to believe. The structural approach of the fractal shows how to juxtapose the most appropriate forms of organi-

The Fractal Factory: the best forms of organization arranged side by side and coordinated with each other

zation in such a way that they are coordinated with each other. It assumes that the current race against time will continue unabated, necessitating a dynamic modification of organizational structures, or the creation of a suitable organizational structure.

In this sense the germ cells of the Fractal Factory are already opening, but it will be a long time before they have united. In the meantime there are a great many questions to be dealt with which could only be touched upon within the scope of this book.

- self-organization
- self-similar goals
- transparency of processes and variables of state
- motivation as the central design principle
- cooperation not confrontation
- internalization of objectives
- quality-consciousness as a matter of course
- competition not restricted to the limits of the company

Fig. 82: Principles of the Fractal Factory

- creation of room for manoeuvre with degrees of freedom
- dynamic organizational structures (evolution)
- self-optimization
- description of processes and depiction of states
- resources are employed as needed
- communication takes place as needed
- entrepreneurial perception, thinking and actions on the part of all staff
- motivational control loop

Fig. 83: Methods of the Fractal Factory

benefits / potentials	greater efficiency	more responsiveness and vitality	faster innovation	conservation of resources
structure	- goal-orientation - self-optimization - self-regulation	- transparency - small control loops - dynamic structure - competition	- self-organization - dynamic structure	
environment	- cooperation	- transparency	- cooperation - market formation	- corporate ethic
workforce	- qualification - teamwork - incentive scheme - self-optimization	- entrepreneurial thinking - qualification	- incentive scheme - entrepreneurial thinking	- corporate ethic - qualification
knowledge	- competence - incentive scheme - information system	- transparency	- dynamic structure - openness	- quality-consciousness - holistic thinking
data	- information system - navigation	- information system		- information system
method	- competence - teamwork	- dynamic structure	- dynamic structure	- competence

Fig. 84: Relationship of potentials, measures and beneficial effects in the Fractal Factory

5. A Glance into the Future

No doubt a great deal of work needs to be done to develop the instrument set we need for the Fractal Factory. But a start has been made. Direct horizontal communication will become more important than the vertical flow of information. The transformation of a function-

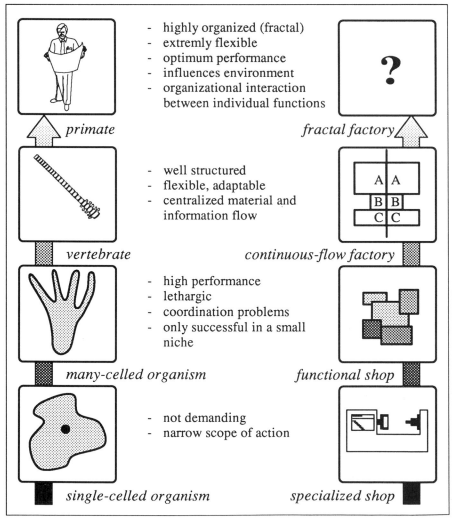

primate

fractal factory

- highly organized (fractal)
- extremly flexible
- optimum performance
- influences environment
- organizational interaction between individual functions

vertebrate

continuous-flow factory

- well structured
- flexible, adaptable
- centralized material and information flow

many-celled organism

functional shop

- high performance
- lethargic
- coordination problems
- only successful in a small niche

single-celled organism

specialized shop

- not demanding
- narrow scope of action

Fig. 85: Evolutionary comparison

oriented, vertically structured organization into a process-oriented, horizontally structured one, tilting it, as it were, through ninety degrees - accompanied by a simultaneous change in management methods in the interests of decentralization and of procedures in the interests of integration - will demand courage and effort. Even when the need has been identified, it is still a big step to put it into practice. There are not yet enough demonstrative examples for us to be sure of the way. And the task is so complex that each factory must find its own way, whereas in such a situation the way itself is in fact the objective.

We must tilt our familiar vertical organization by 90 degrees to obtain horizontal procedures

This book does not purport to provide the reader with a set of instruments which can be put to immediate use in order to bring about tangible improvements in a short time. Nor does the author wish to be counted amongst the host of those offering a patent solution. It is rather my intention to call into question a way of thinking which is deep-rooted in traditional attitudes, and to develop from this a design approach to deal with the tasks we have before us. There are certain to be imperfections and compromises will be necessary. But we need a concept which will be viable in the long term, otherwise we will completely lose our direction in daily practice. Anyone who only ever adopts a new approach when others have provided enough successful examples will always be at the back of the field. We need new visions with new impulses. This purpose is served by the notion of a factory as a living organism. Science and business are developing new ways of looking at the situation and are leaving behind old modes of thinking which offer diminishing marginal utility.

The Fractal Factory: food for thought and an aid to orientation

Do not wait for others. Begin now!

The final image may seem somewhat presumptuous, but perhaps the Fractal Factory will enable us to achieve highly organized structures comparable to those of the primate. One thing is for certain, however: that not even this represents the final stage of evolution.

"Nothing great has ever been achieved without someone dreaming that it should be so, someone believing that it could be so and someone being convinced that it must be so."

Charles F. Kellering

Bibliography

Auch, M.:
Fertigungsstrukturierung auf der Basis von Teilefamilien. Berlin: Springer, 1989. Also Stuttgart: University, thesis, 1989

Barnsley, M.F., Demko, S.:
Fractals everywhere. San Diego: Academic Press, 1988

Beckmann, J.:
Anleitung zur Technologie. Göttingen: Vandenhoeck und Ruprecht, 1796

Blaxill, M.F., Hout, T.M.:
The Fallacy of the Overhead Quick Fix. In: Harvard Business Review (1991) 4, pp. 93-101

Bouillon, H.:
Ordnung, Evolution und Erkenntnis. Hayeks Sozialphilosophie und ihre erkenntnistheoretische Grundlage. Tübingen: Mohr, 1991

Briggs, J., Peat, F.D.:
Turbulent Mirror. New York: Harper & Row, 1989

Brockhaus Encyclopedia:
19th Edition: Mannheim, 1988, Vol. 5, pp. 477-480

Büge, H.:
Anforderungen der Praxis an zukünftige Entgeltsysteme. In: Inst. f. angew. Arbeitswiss. (Ed.): Arbeit: Gestaltung - Organisation - Entgelt. IfaA Publications, Vol. 25. Cologne: Bachem, 1991

Bullinger, H.J.:
Produktionsparadigmen als betriebliche Herausforderung. In: Innovative Unternehmensstrukturen. Berlin: Springer, 1992, pp. 9-25

Christians, F.W.:
Interview. VDI-Nachrichten Magazin (1992) 1, pp. 30-34

Cramer, F.:
Chaos und Ordnung. Die komplexe Struktur des Lebendigen. Stuttgart: DVA, 1989

Crutchfield, J.P.:
Chaos. In: Scientific American 255 (1986) 12, pp. 38-49

Dangelmaier, W., Warnecke, H.J.:
Grenzen der Technik. In: Werkstatttechnik 80 (1990) 3, pp. 145-148

Drucker, P.F.:
The New Realities. New York: Harper & Row, 1989

Drucker, P.F.:
The Emerging Theory of Manufacturing. In: Harvard Business Review (1990) 3, pp. 94-102

Dyson, F.:
Characterizing Irregularity. In: Science 4342 (1978) 12, pp. 677-678

Ederer, G.:
Das leise Lächeln des Siegers. Düsseldorf, Vienna, New York: ECON, 1991

Engel, A.:
Beyond CIM: Bionic Manufacturing Systems in Japan. In: IEEE Expert (1990) 8, pp. 79-81

Engels, F.:
The Condition of the Working Class in England. Oxford: Blackwell, 1958 (translation of the original German text published in 1845)

Eyer, E.:
Anforderungs- und leistungsgerechte Entlohnung in teilautonomen Gruppen. In: Inst. f. angew. Arbeitswiss. (Ed.): Arbeit: Gestaltung - Organisation - Entgelt. IfaA Publications, Vol. 25. Cologne: Bachem, 1991

Ford, H.:
My Life and Work. London: Heinemann, 1922

Franke, H., Buttler, Fr.:
Arbeitswelt 2000. Frankfurt/M.: Fischer 1991

Frey, A.D.:
Luegers Lexikon der gesamten Technik. Stuttgart, Berlin, Leipzig: Deutsche Verlagsanstalt, 1927, Vol. 3, pp. 350-355

Fuchs, J. (Ed.):
Das biokybernetische Modell. Unternehmen als Organismen. Wiesbaden: Gabler, 1992

Haken, H.:
Erfolgsgeheimnisse der Natur. Stuttgart: DVA, 1986

Hacker, W.; Richter, P. (Ed.):
Spezielle Arbeits- und Ingenieurpsychologie in Einzeldarstellungen. Berlin: VEB, 1980

Hammer, H.:
Verfügbarkeitsanalyse von flexiblen Fertigungssystemen. In:
Fertigungstechnisches Kolloquium Stuttgart FTK 1991, Berlin,
Heidelberg, New York: Springer, 1991

Helper, S.:
*How much has really changed between US automakers and their
suppliers?* In: Sloan Management Review 32 (1991) 4, pp. 15-28

Höhler, G.:
Spielregeln für Sieger. Düsseldorf, Vienna, New York, Moscow:
ECON, 1992

Huch, B.:
Eine zielgerichtete Steuerung des Unternehmens. In: Blick durch die
Wirtschaft, 21.1.92, p. 7

Imai, M.:
Kaizen: The Key to Japan's Competitive Success. New York: Random
House, 1986

Institut der deutschen Wirtschaft:
Internationale Wirtschaftszahlen 1991. Cologne: Deutscher Instituts-
Verlag, 1991

Jürgens, U., Malsch, T., Dohse, K.:
Moderne Zeiten in der Automobilfabrik. Berlin: Springer, 1989

Kami, M.J.:
Trigger Points. New York: McGraw-Hill, 1988

KCIM im DIN:
*Fachbericht 15: Normung von Schnittstellen für die rechnerintegrierte
Produktion.* Berlin: Beuth, 1987

Kersten, G.:
*Steuerung und Unterstützung von Produkt- und Prozeßentwicklung
durch Methoden der präventiven Qualitätssicherung.* In: VDI-Z 133
(1991) Special IV, pp. 20-23

Kirchgässner, G.:
*Homo Oeconomicus. Das ökonomische Modell individuellen Verhaltens
und seine Anwendung in den Wirtschafts- und Sozialwissenschaften.*
Tübingen: Mohr, 1991

Kölnische Zeitung 1818:
In: Schönbrunn, G.: *Geschichte in Quellen, das bürgerliche Zeitalter.*
Munich: Bayrischer Schulbuch-Verlag, 1980

Kotter, J.:
A Force for Change - How Leadership Differs from Management. New York, The Free Press 1990

Kühnle, H., Spengler, G.:
Wege in die Fraktale Fabrik. In preparation for io Management-Zeitschrift (to be published 1993)

Manager Magazin 21 (1991) 8, pp. 150-155
Geist auf Vorrat

Mandelbrot, B.:
The fractal Geometry of Nature. San Fransisco: W. H. Freeman, 1982

Mann, R.:
Ein Unternehmen führen heißt offen sein für den Wandel. In: Blick durch die Wirtschaft 205 (1986) pp. 4, 7

Manufacturing Engineering 108 (1992) 1, pp. 31-88
Future View

Maslow, A.H.:
Motivation und Persönlichkeit. Olten: Walter, 1978

Müssigmann, U.:
Bewertung inhomogener fraktaler Strukturen und Skalenanalyse von Texturen. Stuttgart, University, thesis, 1992

Needham, J.:
The Shorter Science and Civilisation in China. Vol 1. Cambridge University Press, Cambridge 1978

Noelle-Neumann, E., Strümpel, B.:
Macht Arbeit krank? Macht Arbeit glücklich? Munich: Piper, 1984

Peitgen, H.O., Richter, P.H.:
The Beauty of Fractals. Berlin: Springer, 1986

Peters, T., Waterman, R.:
In Search of Excellence. New York: Harper & Row, 1982

Peters, T.:
Thriving on Chaos. Handbook for a Management Revolution. London: Macmillan, 1988

Porter, M.E:
Competitive Advantage. New York: The Free Press 1985

Reich, R.:
*The Work of Nations - Preparing Ourselves for 21st-Century
Capitalism.* New York: Knopf, 1991

Riller, P.:
Wege zur recyclingfreundlichen Konstruktion von Elektrogeräten. In:
Produktrücknahme. Auswirkungen, Konsequenzen, Perspektiven.
Frankfurt/M.: Institute for International Research, 1992

Ruppert, W.:
*Die Fabrik - Geschichte von Arbeit und Industrialisierung in
Deutschland.* Munich: Beck, 1983

Rohmert, W.:
*Arbeitswissenschaftliche Beurteilung der Belastung und Beanspruchung
an industriellen Arbeitsplätzen.* Bonn: BMFT, 1975

Scheer, A.W.:
Wirtschaftsinformatik - Informationssysteme im Industriebetrieb.
Berlin, Heidelberg, New York: Springer, 1990

Schiele, O.H.:
Zur Bestimmung des Produktionsstandortes im In- oder Ausland. In:
Schriften zur Unternehmensführung, Vol. 32. Münster: Gabler, 1984

Schiele, O.H.:
Wettbewerbsfähigkeit durch industrielle Automation in der Fertigung.
In: BDI (Ed.): Industrieforschung, Vol. 187. Cologne, 1986

Schiele, O.H.:
*Streiflichter aus 4 Jahrzehnten technischer Entwicklung im
Maschinenbau.* In: VDMA (Ed.): Akzente. Die industrielle
Gemeinschaftsforschung. Cologne, 1992

Schmidtchen, G.:
*Neue Technik, neue Arbeitsmoral. Eine sozialpsychologische
Untersuchung über Motivation in der Metallindustrie.* Cologne: Dt.
Instituts-Verlag, 1984

Schulz, H:
Warum sind erfolgreiche Unternehmen erfolgreich? In: Werkstatt und
Betrieb 124 (1991) 11, pp. 850-851

Schwaninger, M.:
Umweltverantwortung. In: io Management-Zeitschrift 59 (1990) 1,
pp. 89-94

Seitz, K.:
Die japanisch-amerikanische Herausforderung. Munich: Bonn Aktuell,
1991

Senge, P.:
*Fifth Discipline: Mastering the Fifth Practice of the Learning
Organization.* New York: Doubleday, 1990

Sexl, R.U.:
Was die Welt zusammenhält. Frankfurt/M.: Ullstein, 1984

Siebert, H.:
Die Weisheit einer höheren Instanz. In: FAZ March 14,1992, p. 15

Smith, A.:
An Inquiry into the Nature and Causes of the Wealth of Nations.
2 Vols. London: Strahan & Cadell, 1776

Stalk, G., Hout, T.M.:
Competing against Time. New York: The Free Press, 1990

Taylor, F.W.:
The Principles of Scientific Management. New York, London:
W. W. Norton & Co., 1911 reprinted 1967

Ulich, E.:
Arbeitsform mit Zukunft: ganzheitlich-flexibel statt arbeitsteilig. Bern:
Lang, 1989

Wagener, P.:
Arbeitszeitmanagement als Option für Unternehmen und Mitarbeiter.
In: Bundesverband d. dt. Arbeitgeberverb. (Ed.): Leistung und Lohn.
BDA Publications. Bergisch-Gladbach: Heider, 1991

Warnecke, H.J.:
Der Produktionsbetrieb. Berlin, Heidelberg, New York, Tokyo:
Springer, 1993

Wildemann, H.:
*Die modulare Fabrik - Kundennahe Produktion durch
Fertigungssegmentierung.* Munich: gfmt, 1988

Willenbacher, K.:
Die Bedeutung des Institutes für angewandte Arbeitswissenschaften e.V.
In: Inst. f. angew. Arbeitswiss. (Ed.): Arbeit: Gestaltung - Organisation
- Entgelt. IfaA Publications, Vol. 25. Cologne: Bachem, 1991

Womack, J.P., Jones, D.T., Roos, D.:
The Machine that Changed the World. New York: Rawson, 1990

Index